Contents

Front cover: Farebrother's hearse, Kingston-upon-Thames

Introduction

This bibliography is intended primarily for genealogists. It is, however, hoped that it will also prove useful to historians, librarians, archivists, research students, and anyone else interested in the history of Surrey and Sussex. It is intended to be used in conjunction with my *English genealogy: a bibliography,* and the other volumes in the *British genealogical library guides* series. A full list of these volumes currently in print appears on the back cover.

This volume lists published parish registers, monumental inscriptions, and probate records relating to the historic counties of Surrey and Sussex. Volume 1 is devoted to general information on the counties' history, bibliography, archives, journals, *etc.;* other categories of source material for the county are listed in vols. 3-5; pedigrees, family histories, *etc.,* are listed in vol.6. The whole work is exclusively concerned with published works, and thousands of books and journal articles are listed, together with many microfiche publications. However, the innumerable notes and queries to be found in family history society journals *etc.,* are excluded, except where their content is of importance. Where I have included such notes, replies to them are cited in the form 'see also', with no reference to the names of respondents. I have also excluded extracts from newspapers, and works which have not been published. It should be noted that many libraries, such as the Society of Genealogists, hold unpublished transcripts of parish registers, monumental inscriptions, *etc.,* not listed here. Where possible, citations are accompanied by notes indicating the period covered, the locality/ies in which the families concerned dwelt, and other pertinent information. I have physically examined almost every item listed here; those which have not been seen are annotated 'not seen', as I have not been able to check the correct title or the contents.

Be warned: just because information has been published, it does not necessarily follow that it is accurate. I have not made any judgement on the accuracy of most works listed: that is up to you.

Anyone who tries to compile a totally comprehensive bibliography of Surrey and Sussex is likely to fall short of his aim. The task is almost impossible, especially if the endeavour is made by one person. That does not, however, mean that the attempt should not be made. Usefulness, rather than comprehensiveness, has been my prime aim — and this book would not be useful to anyone if its publication were to be prevented by a vain attempt to ensure total comprehensiveness. I am well aware that there are likely to be omissions, especially in view of the fact that, given constraints of time and money, it has not been possible for me to visit all of the large number of libraries with substantial collections on Surrey and Sussex history. Each of them may well possess works not held anywhere else. The identification of such works is not, however, a major aim of this bibliography. Rather, my purpose has been to enable you to identify works which are mostly readily available. Some titles you may be able to purchase; all can be found in libraries throughout the English-speaking world. You can check the holdings of many libraries via their catalogues on the internet; alternatively, if your local library does not hold a particular book, the librarian should be able to tell you where to find it — and, as a last resort, may be able to borrow it for you via the inter-library loan network, irrespective of whether you live in London or San Francisco. The libraries of family history societies are also worth checking — even if they are far distant from Surrey and Sussex: for example, the Genealogical Society of Victoria, in Melbourne, has a good collection of books on English genealogy. Some family history societies offer a postal borrowing service; others may be willing to check a particular book for you. It is also worth joining one of the genealogical newsgroups or mailing lists on the internet; other members may hold the books you need, and be willing to check them for you.

If you are an assiduous researcher, you may well come across items I have missed. If you do, please let me know, so that they can be included in the next edition.

The work of compiling this bibliography has depended heavily on the resources of the libraries I have used. These included the Surrey History Centre, and local studies collections in the public libraries of Worthing, Chichester, Brighton, Eastbourne, Hastings, Richmond, Brixton, Croydon, and Southwark, as well as West Sussex Record Office. I have also relied heavily on the Society of Genealogists, the University of Exeter, Exeter Public Library, the British Library, and the Society of Genealogists, All these institutions deserve my thanks, as do Cliff Webb and Martin Hayes, who both read and commented on an early draft of the book. Cynthia Hanson typed the manuscript, and Bob Boyd saw the book through the press. I am grateful too to the officers of the Federation of Family History Societies, whose support is vital for the continuation of this series. My thanks also to my wife Marjorie.

Stuart A. Raymond

Abbreviations

B.R.L.H.S.N.	Bognor Regis Local History Society newsletter
D.P.H.S.M.	Danehill Parish Historical Society magazine
E.L.H.	Eastbourne Local Historian
E.L.H.S.N.	Eastbourne Local History Society newsletter
E.Sy.F.H.S.J.	East Surrey Family History Society journal
F.M.S.Q.N.	Farnham Museum Society quarterly newsletter
F.H.S.	Family History Society
F.R.	Family Roots
H. & R.F.H.S.J.	Hastings & Rother Family History Society [journal]
L.H.R.	Local history records for Caterham and Warlingham, Coulsdon and Purley [Bourne Society local history records]
M.G.H.	Miscellanea genealogica et heraldica
N.S.	New Series
P.L.D.L.H.S.	Proceedings of the Leatherhead & District Local History Society
P.R.S.	Parish Register Society
R. & B.	Root and branch [West Surrey F.H.S. journal]
R.H.	Richmond history
Sx.A.C	Sussex archaeological collections
Sx.A.S.N.	Sussex Archaeological Society newsletter
Sx.F.H.	Sussex family historian
Sx.G.L.H.	Sussex genealogist and local historian
Sx.N.Q.	Sussex notes and queries
Sx.R.S.	Sussex Record Society
Sy.A.C.	Surrey archaeological collections
Sy.R.S.	Surrey Record Society
W.Sx.H.	West Sussex history

Bibliographic Presentation

Authors names are in SMALL CAPITALS. Book and journal titles are in *italics*. Articles appearing in journals, and material such as parish register transcripts, forming only part of books are in inverted commas and textface type. Volume numbers are in **bold** and the individual number of the journal may be shown in parentheses. These are normally followed by the place of publication (except where this is London, which is omitted), the name of the publisher and the date of publication. In the case of articles, further figures indicate page numbers.

Libraries and Record Offices

There are numerous libraries with substantial book collections relating to Surrey and Sussex. For the present (post-1974) county of Surrey, the major library is the Surrey History Centre; however, boundary changes mean that there are also 6 London metropolitan boroughs in historic Surrey, all of which have specialist local history collections. Most public libraries also have some local history materials.

For Sussex, most of the major town libraries have substantial local history collections, as do the Record Offices of East and West Sussex. The libraries at Worthing and Brighton probably have the most substantial collections.

Collections relating to Surrey and Sussex may also be found in many other public and university libraries throughout the country (and, indeed, the world), as well as at specialist institutions such as the Society of Genealogists and the British Library. The local family history societies also have small libraries.

The list which follows concentrates on those libraries within the historic counties, and is very selective.

SURREY

Surrey History Centre,
130, Goldsworth Road,
Woking,
Surrey, GU21 1ND

Croydon
Croydon Library & Archives
 Service,
Katharine Street,
Croydon,
Surrey, CR9 1ET

Kingston on Thames
Local History Centre,
Heritage Centre,
Wheatfield Way,
Kingston on Thames,
Surrey, KT1 2PS

Lambeth
Minet Library,
52, Knatchbull Road,
Brixton,
London, SE5 9QY

Merton
Merton Local Studies Centre,
Merton Civic Centre,
London Road,
Morden,
Surrey, SM4 5DX

Richmond
Richmond Local Studies Library,
Central Reference Library,
Old Town Hall,
Whittaker Avenue,
Richmond,
Surrey, TW9 1TP

Southwark
Southwark Local Studies Library,
211, Borough High Street,
Southwark,
London, SE1 1JA

Sutton
Sutton Archives,
Central Library,
St. Nicholas Way,
Sutton,
Surrey, SM1 1EA

Wandsworth
Wandsworth Local History
  Collection,
Battersea Library,
265, Lavender Hill
London, SW11 1JB

SUSSEX

East Sussex Record Office,
The Maltings,
Castle Precincts,
Lewes,
Sussex, BN7 1YT

West Sussex Record Office,
County Hall,
Chichester,
PO19 1RN

Brighton
Brighton Local Studies Library,
Church Street,
Brighton,
Sussex, BN1 1UD

Chichester
Local Studies Collection,
West Sussex County Library,
Tower Street,
Chichester,
Sussex, PO19 1QJ

Eastbourne
Local Studies Collection,
Eastbourne Library,
Grove Road,
Eastbourne,
Sussex, BN21 4LT

Hastings

Local Studies Collection,
Hastings Library,
Brassey Institute,
13, Claremont,
Hastings, TN34 1HE

Lewes

Sussex Room,
Lewes Library,
Albion Street,
Lewes,
Sussex, BN7 2ND

Worthing

Local Studies Library.
Worthing Library,
Richmond Road,
Worthing,
Sussex, BN11 1HD

1. PARISH REGISTERS

Parish registers are vital sources of information for genealogists researching ancestry in the nineteenth century and earlier. In order to locate those for Surrey and Sussex, you need to consult the relevant volumes of the *National index of parish registers*. See:

PALGRAVE-MOOR, PATRICK T.R. *National index of parish registers ... vol.IV: South East England. Kent, Surrey and Sussex.* Society of Genealogists, 1980.

This volume is now rather dated, and the Surrey section has been replaced by:

WEBB, CLIFF. *National index of parish registers... volume 4, part 1. Surrey.* Society of Genealogists, 1990. The locations given in this volume are likely to be wrong, since the Surrey History Centre has amalgamated the collections of several major Surrey repositories.

See also:

WEBB, CLIFF. *Guide to Surrey bishops' transcripts, marriage licence allegations and probate records.* 4th ed. Research series **11**. West Surrey F.H.S., 1999.

There are a number of guides to Surrey registers in particular repositories:

HARRIS, T.C. *Guide to parish registers deposited in the Greater London Record Office.* 2nd ed. Greater London Record Office, 1991. Includes registers for Battersea, Bermondsey, Camberwell, Deptford, Lambeth, and Wandsworth.

A survey of the parish registers of the Diocese of Southwark. Inner London area. 2nd ed. Great London Record Office, 1970. Covers Battersea, Bermondsey, Camberwell, Clapham & Brixton, Deptford, Dulwich, Lambeth, Southwark & Newington, Streatham, Tooting and Wandsworth deaneries.

Guide to parish registers held at County Hall, Kingston, and in the Guildford Muniment Room. Surrey County Council, 1993.

SUTTON HERITAGE SERVICE. *Guide to copies of Surrey parish registers.* Sutton: Archive & Local Studies Department, [199-?] List of fiche transcripts, *etc.,* held at Sutton Central Library.

WEBB, CLIFF. 'Guildford Diocese (West Surrey) parish registers', *E.Sy.F.H.S.J.* **12**(1), 1989, 31-34. List of transcripts held by the compiler.

WEBB, CLIFF. 'Southwark Diocese (East Surrey) parish registers', *E.Sy.F.H.S.J.* **11**(3), 1988, 34-6. List of modern transcripts held by the compiler.

Surrey indexes available include:

BENNY, ALAN. *East Surrey burials index, 1813-1840.* 2 fiche in folder. East Surrey F.H.S. microfiche series **29**. 2000.

BENNY, ALAN. *West Surrey burial index, 1813-1840.* 2 fiche in folder. Microfiche series **25**. West Surrey F.H.S., 1998.

WEBB, CLIFF. *West Surrey burial index, 1841-1865: first edition - partial index (over 20,000 entries).* 2 fiche in folder. W.Surrey F.H.S., microfiche series, **15**. 1994.

COOKE, B. CAMPBELL. 'List of transcripts of Surrey parish registers', *Sy.A.C.* **46**, 1938, 114-24. See also **47**, 1941, 103.

'Selon index', *E.Sy.F.H.S.J.* **6**(2), 1983, 16-18. See also **9**(3), 1986, 33, & **11**(1), 1988, 32. List of parishes in Southwark and Bermondsey covered by the *Selon* index of parish registers *etc.*

WEBB, CLIFF. *Surrey super index to non-Metropolitan parish records.* 3rd ed. 3 fiche in folder. West Surrey F.H.S., microfiche series **4**. 2000. Primarily an index to the Society's indexes of parish registers.

'Entries of Kentish interest in Surrey parish registers', *Family history: the journal of the Institute of Heraldic and Genealogical Studies* **8**(43/45); N.S., **19/21**, 1973, 96-107. From Addington, Chelsham, Chipstead, Farleigh, Gatton, Sanderstead, Tatsfield, Titsey, Warlingham and Woldingham.

MCGOWAN, ALAN. 'Hampshire strays in Surrey', *Hampshire family historian* **12**(1), 1985, 42-4; **12**(3), 1985, 149-51.

For Sussex registers, see:

A handlist of registers of births, baptisms, marriages, deaths and burials. Lewes: East Sussex County Council, 1995.

Handlist of Sussex parish register copies in the library of the Sussex Family History Group. Brighton: Sussex Family History Group, 1977. Additions regularly appear in *Sx.F.H.*

Diocese of Chichester: a handlist of the Bishops' transcripts, 1567-1936. Chichester: West Sussex County Council, 1970.

TEVIOT, LORD & LADY. *Guide to Sussex burial index, 1813-1837. Vol. 1: Eastern Sussex.* [The authors], [1989?]

TEVIOT, LORD & LADY. 'Indexers and their indexes: the Sussex burial index 1813-1837', *Family tree magazine* 8(9), 1992, 19.

Other works on Sussex registers include:

ARSCOTT, DAVID. *What the vicar saw.* Westmeston: Pomegranate Press, 1999. Cover: 'Gloriously indiscreet gleanings from the Sussex parish registers'.

BLENCOWE, ROBERT WILLIS. 'Extracts from the parish registers and other parochial documents of East Sussex', *Sx.A.C.* 4, 1851, 243-90. General discussion.

BURCHALL, MICHAEL JOHN. *Sussex military marriages, 1750-1812.* Brighton: Manuscripts of Sussex, for Sussex Family History Group 1975.

CAPLAN, NEIL. 'Registers discovered', *Sx.F.H.* 4(1), 1979, 19-20. Brief discussion.

CHALLEN, W.H. 'Parish registers and bishops transcripts: Archdeaconry of Chichester', *Sx.N.Q.* 10, 1944-5, 27-33, 56-7, 82-15, 100-101, 128-31, 150-53, 174-7 & 193-9. List, including list of Challen's own transcripts.

CHALLEN, W.H. 'Bishops transcripts: Archdeaconries of Lewes and Hastings', *Sx.N.Q.* 10, 1944-5, 9-13. Lists, with list of Challen's own transcripts.

RENSHAW, W.C. 'Bishops transcripts for the Archdeaconry of Lewes', *Sx.A.C.* 55, 1912, 314. List of bishops transcripts earlier in date than the earliest registers.

Non-Conformist Register

A variety of fiche, books and articles relating to non-conformist registers are available:

Surrey non-conformist registers. Microfiche series 5. 2 fiche in folder. West Surrey F.H.S., 1990. Transcripts of registers with index.

BURGESS, WALTER H. 'Sussex non-parochial registers and records', *Sussex county magazine* 16, 1942, 69-72. General discussion, with list.

CAPLAN, N. 'Sussex non-parochial registers', *Sx.N.Q.* 15, 1958-62, 334-8. General discussion of the registers as historical sources.

Methodist

O'SULLIVAN, MAUREEN, & POATE, WYN. *Wesleyan Methodist Metropolitan Registry 1818-1840.* Record publication M61. E.Sy.F.H.S., 1997.

Presbyterians, etc.

O'SULLIVAN, MAUREEN. *Dr. Williams' Library: the Presbyterian, Independent and Baptist Registry. Surrey extracts. Baptism 8 Apr. 1743 (birth 19 Jan. 1732) to baptism 30 Dec. 1837 (birth 13 Oct. 1799).* 9 fiche in folder. East Surrey F.H.S. record publication 62. 1997.

Quaker

LUCAS, PERCEVAL. 'Some notes on the early Sussex Quaker registers', *Sx.A.C.* 55, 1912, 74-96. Notes on 10 registers deposited at the Public Record Office.

Roman Catholic

MCCANN, TIMOTHY. 'A survey of Sussex catholic registers', *Sx.G.L.H.* 6(3), 1984, 93-7. Includes list.

MCCANN, TIMOTHY J. *West Sussex Catholic registers: baptisms 1698-1800.* [ ]: Sussex Family History Group, 1998.

MCCANN, T.J. 'Sussex catholic registers', *E.C.A.[English catholic ancestor] journal* 2(3), 1987, 67-9. Includes list.

Marriage Licences

Surrey

BAX, ARNOLD RIDLEY. *Commissary Court of Surrey allegations for marriage licences 1662-1665; 1674-1770.* Microfiche series 26. West Surrey F.H.S., 1997. Originally published 1907.

BAX, ALFRED RIDLEY, ed. *Allegations for marriage licences issued by the Commissary Court of Surrey between 1673-1770 ...* 3 vols. Norwich: Goose & Sons, 1907.

BAX, ALFRED RIDLEY. 'Marriage and other licences in the Commissary Court of Surrey', *Sy.A.C.* 11, 1893, 204-43. 1662-5.

LONDON METROPOLITAN ARCHIVES. *Diocese of Winchester: Archdeaconry of Surrey. Index to marriage bonds and allegations 1770-1850 (part).* 6 fiche. London Metropolitan Archives, 2000.

WEBB, CLIFF. 'Surrey marriage licences in the *annus mirabilis, R. & B.* **13**(1), 1986, 25-6., **13**(2), 1986, 59-61. For 1822-3.

Sussex

DUNKIN, EDWIN H.W., ed. *Calendar of Sussex marriage licences recorded in the Consistory Court of the Bishop of Chichester for the Archdeaconry of Chichester, June 1575 to December 1730.* Sx.R.S. **9**. 1909.

DUNKIN, EDWIN H.W. *Calendar of Sussex marriage licences recorded in the Consistory Court of the Bishop of Chichester January 1731 to December 1774,* ed. D. Macleod. Sx.R.S. **32**. 1926.

DUNKIN, EDWIN H. *Calendar of Sussex marriage licences recorded in the Consistory Court of the Bishop of Chichester for the Archdeaconry of Chichester, January 1775 to December 1800,* ed. D.Macleod. Sx.R.S. **35**. 1929. Includes 'index to vols. XXXII and XXXV, 1731-1800'.

DUNKIN, EDWIN H.W., ed. *Calendar of Sussex marriage licences recorded in the Consistory Court of the Bishop of Chichester for the Archdeaconry of Lewes, August 1586 to March 1642-3.* Sx.R.S. **1**. 1901.

DUNKIN, EDWIN H.W., ed. *Calendar of Sussex marriage licences recorded in the Consistory Court of the Bishop of Chichester for the Archdeaconry of Lewes, August 1670 to March 1728-9, and in the peculiar court of the Archbishop of Canterbury for the Deanery of South Malling, May 1620 to December 1732.* Sx.R.S. **6**. 1907. Corrected in:

'Lewes licences 1685', *Sx.F.H.* **3**(6), 1978, 179-80.

DUNKIN, EDWIN H. *Calendar of Sussex marriage licences recorded in the Consistory Court of the Bishop of Chichester for the Archdeaconry of Lewes, and in the peculiar court of the Archbishop of Canterbury for the

Deanery of South Malling 1772-1837, ed. E.W.D.Penfold. 2 vols. Sx.R.S. **25-6**. 1917-19.

DUNKIN, EDWIN H.W., ed. *Calendar of Sussex marriage licences recorded in the peculiar courts of the Dean of Chichester and of the Archbishop of Canterbury. Deanery of Chichester January 1582-3 to December 1730. Deaneries of Pagham and Tarring, January 1579-80 to November 1730.* Sx.R.S. **12**. 1911.

For unpublished transcripts of E.H.Dunkin, which continue his Sussex Record Society volumes to 1837, see:

LEESON, FRANK. 'Unpublished West Sussex marriage licences', *Sx.F.H.* **6**(4), 1984, 144.

Other brief extracts include:

LEESON, FRANK. 'The *annus mirabilis* in Sussex', *Sx.F.H.* **6**(1), 1984, 28-9; **6**(2), 1984, 64-5; **6**(3), 1984, 106-7; **6**(5), 1985, 186-8. Marriage licence allegations 1822-3.

HUDSON, MARGARET, 'Allegations for marriage licences, 1669-1679: Sussex parties', *Sx.F.H.* **5**(5), 1983, 144-9. Issued by the Vicar General of the Archbishop of Canterbury.

Funeral Records

LONGLEY, R.A. *Funerals carried out by Stuart Horsler's Ltd., 1949-[1981].* 4 vols. St.Leonards on Sea: R.A.Longley, 1998. Horsler's were funeral directors. Volumes cover 1949-64, 1964-70, 1970-76, & 1976-81.

Newspaper Announcements

SAUNDERS, JACK. 'Surrey B, M & D announcements', *E.Sy.F.H.S.J.* **3**(3), 1980, 20-21. In the *Croydon guardian* for 27 Oct.1877, 25 Feb.1882, 4 March 1882, 15 July 1882, and 22 July, 1882.

Index to births, marriages, deaths, and in memoria notices in the Sutton and Epsom Advertiser & Surrey County Reporter, 1882-1886 & 1888-1893, and Croydon Advertiser 1887. 4 fiche in folder. East Surrey F.H.S. record publications **41**. 1993.

DEVONSHIRE, MARY. 'Surrey entries in *The European magazine and London review,* 1822', *E.Sy.F.H.S.J.* **18**(4), 1995, 20-23. Bankrupts, insolvents, births, marriages and deaths, *etc.*

CRIDDLE, MAUREEN. 'Surrey entries in *The Folkestone chronicle,* 1856-1858', *E.Sy.F.H.S.J.* **18**(4), 1995, 24.

Strays

CHALLEN, W.H. 'Sussex entries in London parish registers', *Sx.N.Q.* **1-16**, 1926-63, *passim.* Numerous brief extracts from many London registers.

WAKELIN, W.G. 'Strays in Hampshire', *Sx.F.H.* **3**(6), 1978, 190-1. From marriage register, 17-19th c., also a few 19th c. inscriptions.

CHALLEN, W.H. 'Sussex entries in Surrey registers', *Sx.A.C.* **70**, 1929, 213-6. Extracts from the registers of Banstead, Headley, Walton on the Hill, and Streatham.

CHRISTMAS, BRIAN. 'Your missing link?', R. & B. **14**(2), 1987, 54-6. Entries from the registers of St. George's Chapel, Windsor, relating to Surrey, 1675-1945.

FRY, GEORGE S. 'Dorset marriage licences', *Notes and queries for Somerset and Dorset* **15**, 1917, 58. In Surrey.

HADAWAY, MAISIE J. 'Sussex strays from Stone-in-Oxney P.Rs', *Sx.F.H.* **8**(4), 1988, 157-8. 16-20th c.

'Sussex strays from Stone-in-Oxney P.Rs', *H. &.R.F.H.S.J.* **5**(1), 1990, 21-2. 16-20th c.

'Sussex strays from Stone in Oxney, Kent', **7**(6), 1987, 244-5. From the parish register, 17-20th c.

SURREY
Abinger

The parish registers of Abinger, Wotton, and Oakwood Chapel, Co.Surrey. Sy.R.S. **[9]**. 1927. Also issued as no. **25** of the Society's publications. Coverage is as follows: Abinger baptisms and burials 1559-1806, marriages 1559-1755, additional banns, 1653-8 and 1754-1812. Wotton baptisms and burials 1596-1812, marriages 1653-1751, additional banns 1755-1812. Oakwood Chapel baptisms 1700-1814, marriages 1697-1751, burials 1696-1813. Also includes lists of Abinger and Wotton rectors. Reprinted, with additions for 1813-1840, in:

The parish registers of Abinger, Wotton, and Oakwood, Surrey: transcript and indexes. 5 microfiche in folder. Parish registers on microfiche series **1**. West Surrey F.H.S., 1993.

Addington

BANNERMAN, W. BRUCE. ed. *The parish registers of Addington, Co.Surrey.* Surrey P.R.S., **5**. 1907. Bound with the registers of Chelsham, and Warlingham, 1559-1812.

Addington: parish church of St. Mary the Blessed Virgin. Baptisms 1813-1851; marriages 1813-1837. Record publication **M19**. East Surrey F.H.S., 1995.

S[TEINMAN], G.S. 'Extracts from the registers of Addington, Co.Surrey', *Collectanea topographica et genealogica* **7**, 1841, 286-91.

Addlestone
See Egham

Albury

WEBB, CLIFF, et al, eds. *Albury, Surrey, baptisms 1559-1840; marriages, 1559-1733; burials 1559-1840.* 2 fiche in folder. West Surrey F.H.S., 1999.

Alfold

WEBB, CLIFF, et al, eds. *Alfold, Surrey: baptisms 1658-1841; burials 1658-1840.* 1 fiche in folder. West Surrey F.H.S., 1999.

Ash

WEBB, CLIFF, MESLEY, BOB, et al, eds. *Ash, Surrey: baptisms 1558-1840; marriages 1550-1837; banns 1781-1803, 1823; burials 1559-1840.* 2 fiche in folder. West Surrey F.H.S., 1999.

Ashtead

WEBB, CLIFF, et al, eds. *Ashtead, Surrey: baptisms 1662-1840; burials 1662-1840.* 2 fiche in folder. West Surrey F.H.S., 1995.

Banstead

LAMBERT, F.A. HEYGATE, ed. *The register of Banstead in the County of Surrey 1547-1789.* Parish Register Society **1**. 1896. Reprinted with additions, in:

WEBB, CLIFF, et al, eds. *Banstead, Surrey: baptisms 1547-1840; marriages 1547-1753; burials 1548-1840.* 1 fiche in folder. West Surrey F.H.S., 1998.

Beddington

BANNERMAN, W.B., ed. *The parish registers of Beddington, Co.Surrey.* Surrey P.R.S., **10**. 1912. For 1538-1673. Bound with the register of Morden. Reprinted, with additions, in:

WEBB, CLIFF. et al, eds. *Beddington, Surrey: baptisms 1561-1840; marriages 1538-1671; burials 1538-1840.* 2 fiche in folder. West Surrey F.H.S., 1999.

Bermondsey

The parish registers of St. Mary Magdalene, Bermondsey, 1548-1609. Exeter: William Pollard & Co., 1894. Supplement to the *Genealogist.*

MOYNIHAN, A.B., & MOYNIHAN, A.M. *Dockhead Roman Catholic parish of Bermondsey, Surrey. East Lane Chapel/the Most Holy Trinity. Parish registers 1801-1854.* 5 fiche in folder. East Surrey F.H.S. record publication 59. [199-.]

WEBB, CLIFF. 'Boards of Guardians [Workhouse] registers for Surrey metropolitan parishes', *R. & B.* 17(4), 1991, 138-9. List of birth, death, and marriage registers for Bermondsey, Camberwell, Lambeth, Southwark, and Wandsworth, 19-20th c.

Betchworth

WEBB, CLIFF, ed. *Betchworth, Surrey: baptisms 1556-1840; burials 1558-1840.* 2 fiche in folder. West Surrey F.H.S., 1999.

Bisley

WEBB, CLIFF. et al, eds. *Bisley, Surrey: baptisms 1561-1840; marriages, 1561-1837; burials 1561-1851.* 2 fiche in folder. West Surrey F.H.S., 1995.

Burstow

WEBB, CLIFF. et al, eds. *Burstow, Surrey: christenings & burials 1547-1840.* 1 fiche. West Surrey F.H.S., 2000. Not seen.

Byfleet

WEBB, CLIFF, et al, eds. *Byfleet, Surrey: baptisms 1698-1840; burials 1728-1840.* 1 fiche in folder. West Surrey F.H.S., 1995.

Camberwell

S[TEINMAN], G.S. 'Extracts from the parish registers of Camberwell, Surrey', *Collectanea topographica et genealogica* 3, 1836, 142-68.
See also Bermondsey

Capel

CARTER, HECTOR, ed. *Capel, Surrey: baptisms, 1653-1840; marriages, 1653-1840; burials, 1653-1840.* 2 fiche in folder. West Surrey F.H.S., 1996.

Caterham

BANNERMAN, W. BRUCE, ed. *The parish registers of Caterham, in the county of Surrey.* Surrey P.R.S., 14-15. 1917-18.

Cheam

HANSOM, J.S., ed. 'The Catholic registers of Cheam in Surrey', in *Miscellanea* II. Catholic Record Society 2. 1906, 314-37. 1755-1787.

Chelsham

BANNERMAN, W. BRUCE, ed. *The parish registers of Chelsham, Co.Surrey.* Surrey P.R.S., 5. 1907, 1669-1812. Bound with the registers for Addington and Warlingham.

Chertsey

WEBB, CLIFF, SYKES, AUDREY, et al, eds. *Chertsey, Surrey baptisms, c.1620-1840; marriages 1607-1693; burials 1607-1840.* 4 fiche in folder. West Surrey F.H.S., 1999.

MESLEY, ROBERT. 'Chertsey dissenters register', *R. & B.* 24(2), 1997, 58-62. Baptism 1758-1864; burials 1783-1865.

Chiddingfold

WILCOCK, TIM, WEBB, CLIFF, et al, eds. *Chiddingfold, Surrey: baptisms 1573-1575; 1595-1840; marriages 1563-1837; burials 1563-1840.* 2 fiche in folder. West Surrey F.H.S., 1999.

Chipstead

BANNERMAN, W. BRUCE, ed. *The parish registers of Chipstead, Co.Surrey.* Surrey P.R.S., 7. 1909. Bound with the register for Titsey. 1656-1812. Reprinted with additions in:

WEBB, CLIFF, ed. *Chipstead, Surrey: baptisms 1656-1841; marriages, 1643-1812; burials 1651-1841. Pre-1812 from the printed edition of 1909.* 1 fiche in folder. West Surrey F.H.S., 1995.

Chobham

WEBB, CLIFF, et al, eds. *Chobham, Surrey.*
Baptisms 1587-1588, 1654-1840; marriages
1587-1588, 1729; burials 1587-1588, 1654-
1840. 3 fiche in folder. West Surrey F.H.S.,
1996.

Cobham

Cobham, Surrey. Christenings 1562-1565,
1610-1840. Burials 1562-1563; 1610-1840. 2
fiche in folder. West Surrey F.H.S., 2000.
Not seen.

Compton

WEBB, CLIFF, et al, eds. *Compton, Surrey:*
baptisms, 1587, 1639-1840; marriages, 1587;
burials, 1587; 1639-1840. 1 fiche in folder.
West Surrey F.H.S., 1995.
WEBB, CLIFF. 'Compton: Various lists of
names 1810-1821', *R. & B.* **23**(3), 1996, 98-
100. Various lists found in the parish
register, including persons inoculated or
vaccinated, and confirmees etc.

Coulsdon

BANNERMAN, W. BRUCE, ed. *The parish*
registers of Coulsdon, Co.Surrey. Surrey
P.R.S., **8**. 1910. Also published as Parish
Register Society **75**. Bound with the
register for Haslemere.
BROADBENT, UNA. 'Coulsdon parish registers
1653-1812', *L.R.H.* **15**, 1976, 14-18. General
discussion.
St. John the Evangelist, Coulsdon, Surrey,
Diocese of Southwark ... indexes to
baptisms, 1813-1856. 1 fiche in folder. East
Surrey F.H.S. record publication **52**. [199-].
St. John the Evangelist, Coulsdon, Surrey,
Diocese of Southwark ... Indexes to
marriages 1813-1915. 1 fiche in folder.
East Surrey F.H.S. record publication **53**.
[199-.]
Coulsdon, Surrey: burials 1813-1879. 1 fiche
in folder. East Surrey F.H.S. record
publication **54**. [199-].

Cranleigh

WEBB, CLIFF, MESLEY, BOB, et al, eds.
Cranleigh, Surrey: baptisms 1566-1567,
1608-1840; marriages 1609-1837; burials
1609-1840. 3 fiche. West Surrey F.H.S.,
1999.

Crowhurst

WEBB, CLIFF, et al, eds. *Crowhurst, baptisms*
1567-1840; marriages 1573-1677, 1706-1712,
1732-1749; burials 1567-1681, 1702-1843.
1 fiche in folder. West Surrey F.H.S., 1999.

Croydon

GALLAGHER, SHEILA. 'Strangers in Croydon',
E.Sy.F.H.S.J. **17**(1), 1994, 37. List of burials
1830-34 from the registers of St.James,
Croydon.
O'SULLIVAN, MAUREEEN. *Croydon, Surrey.*
St. James' church baptisms 1829-51 & 1851-
1906 (extracts). East Surrey F.H.S. record
publication. **4**. 1987.
O'SULLIVAN, MAUREEN. *Croydon, Surrey. St.*
James' church burials, 1829-1866. 1 fiche.
East Surrey F.H.S. record publication, **5**.
1987.
S[TEINMAN], G.S. 'Extracts from the parish
registers of Croydon, Surrey', *Collectanea*
topographica et genealogica **2**, 1835,
292-6. Includes a few monumental
inscriptions.
S[TEINMAN], G.S. 'Further extracts from the
parish registers of Croydon', *Collectanea*
topographica et genealogica **3**, 1836, 307-8;
4, 1837, 91-5.

Dorking

WEBB, CLIFF, et al, eds. *Dorking, Surrey:*
baptisms & burials, 1538-1840, and
Holmwood: baptisms & burials 1838-1840.
5 fiche in folder. West Surrey F.H.S., 1999.

Dunsfold

WEBB, CLIFF, et al, eds. *Dunsfold, Surrey:*
baptisms 1587-1588; 1628-1840; marriages
1588, 1628-1640. 1 fiche in folder. West
Surrey F.H.S., 1999.

East Clandon

SYKES, AUDREY, & WEBB, CLIFF, et al, eds.
East Clandon, Surrey: baptisms 1558-1840,
burials 1559-1840. 1 fiche in folder. West
Surrey F.H.S., 1995.

East Horsley

WEBB, CLIFF, et al, eds. *East Horsley, Surrey:*
baptisms 1666-1840; marriages 1667-1837;
burials 1666-1840. 1 fiche in folder. West
Surrey F.H.S., 1995.

East Molesey

WEBB, CLIFF, et al, eds. *East Molesey, Surrey: baptisms 1668-1840; burials 1681-1840.* 2 fiche in folder. West Surrey F.H.S., 1995.

Effingham

WEBB, CLIFF, et al, eds. *Effingham, Surrey: baptisms, 1565-1851; marriages, 1565-1837; burials, 1565-1852.* 3 fiche in folder. West Surrey F.H.S. 1995.

Egham

SYKES, AUDREY, CARTER, HECTOR, MESLEY, BOB, & WEBB, CLIFF, et al, eds. *Egham, Surrey: baptisms 1560-1840; marriages 1653-1752; burials, 1592-1840, with Addlestone baptisms and burials 1838-1840, and Virginia Water baptisms 1838-1840, burials 1839-1865.* 4 fiche. West Surrey F.H.S., 1999.

Esher

WEBB, CLIFF, et al, eds. *Esher, Surrey: baptisms 1679, 1682-1840; marriage (1 only) 1685; burials 1678-1841.* 2 fiche in folder. West Surrey F.H.S., 1998.

Ewhurst

SYKES, AUDREY. WEBB, CLIFF, et al, eds. *Ewhurst, Surrey: baptisms 1587, 1614-1840; marriages 1614-1720; burials 1587-1588, 1614-1840.* 1 fiche in folder. West Surrey F.H.S., 1999.

Farleigh

RICE, R. GARRAWAY, ed. *The registers of Farleigh in the County of Surrey.* Surrey P.R.S. 4. 1906. 1678-1812; includes monumental inscriptions and briefs. Bound with the registers of Tatsfield, Wanborough and Woldingham.

Farnham

PARKS, PEGGY. 'Marriages in the chapel of Farnham Castle, 1729-1758', *F.M.S.Q.N.* 7(4), 1984, 92-6. Extracts from Farnham parish registers, and from allegations for licences.

PARNELL, SHIRLEY. 'Military baptisms at Farnham, 1801-1840', *R. & B.* 8(1), 1981, 25-6.

PARNELL, SHIRLEY. 'Londoners baptised at St. Andrew's, Farnham, 1801-40', *R. & B.* 4(3), 1978, 102.

'Adult baptisms at Farnham 1801-1840', *R. & B.* 5(3), 1979, 91. From the register of St. Andrews.

MCGOWAN, ALAN. 'More late baptisms at Farnham, 1841-1863', *R. & B.* 5(4), 1979, 132.

Fetcham

WEBB, CLIFF, et al, eds. *Fetcham, Surrey: baptisms 1559-1840; burials 1562-1840.* 1 fiche in folder. West Surrey F.H.S., 1995.

LEWARNE, J.G.W. 'Fetcham parish registers', *P.L.D.L.H.S.* 1(8), 1954, 6-10. Description.

Frensham

Frensham, Surrey: christenings 1650-1840; burials 1649-1840. 2 fiche in folder. West Surrey F.H.S., 1997. Not seen.

Frimley

WEBB, CLIFF, & MESLEY, BOB, et al, eds. *Frimley, Surrey: baptisms 1589-1840; burials 1606-1840.* 2 fiche in folder. West Surrey F.H.S., 1995.

Gatton

BANNERMAN, W. BRUCE, ed. *The parish registers of Gatton, Co.Surrey.* Surrey P.R.S. 6. 1908. 1599-1812. Bound with the register for Sanderstead.

Godalming

MALDEN, HENRY C., ed. *The parish registers of Godalming, Surrey.* Surrey P.R.S. 2. 1904. 1582-1688. Reprinted on 6 fiche, West Surrey F.H.S., [199-?] Reprinted with additions in:

WEBB, CLIFF. *Godalming, Surrey: baptisms 1582-1840; marriages 1583-1837; burials 1583-1840.* 6 fiche in folder. West Surrey F.H.S., [199-].

Godstone

WEBB, CLIFF, et al, eds. *Godstone, Surrey: baptisms 1662-1840; burials 1662-1840.* 1 fiche in folder. West Surrey F.H.S., 1999.

Great Bookham

WEBB, CLIFF, MESLEY, BOB, et al, eds. *Great Bookham, Surrey: baptisms 1632-1840; marriages 1632-1837; burials 1632-1840.* 2 fiche in folder. West Surrey F.H.S., 1999.

Guildford

ANDERSON, AUDREY, WEBB, CLIFF, et al, eds. *Guildford, Surrey: Holy Trinity - St. Mary - St. Nicholas: baptisms 1813-1840; burials 1813-1840.* 1 fiche in folder. West Surrey F.H.S., 1999.

SYKES, AUDREY, WEBB, CLIFF, et al, eds. *St. Nicholas, Guildford, Surrey: baptisms 1561-1812; marriages 1561-1754; burials 1561-1812.* 2 fiche in folder. West Surrey F.H.S., 1999.

MESLEY, BOB. 'Stray marriages in Guildford', *R. & B.* **23**(4), 1997, 142-3. General discussion, not a list.

Hambledon

WEBB, CLIFF, ed. *Hambledon, Surrey: baptisms, 1587, 1617-1840; burials, 1587, 1617-1865.* 1 fiche in folder. West Surrey F.H.S., 1999.

Hascombe

WEBB, CLIFF, MESLEY, BOB, et al, eds. *Hascombe, Surrey: baptisms 1588, 1646-1840; burials 1659-1865.* 1 fiche in folder. West Surrey F.H.S., 1998.

Haslemere

PENFOLD, JOHN WORNHAM. *The parish registers of Haslemere, Co.Surrey. 1573-1812.* Surrey P.R.S. **8-9**. 1910. Bound with the registers for Coulsdon. (vol.8) and Stoke D'Abernon (vol.9) Reprinted with additions in:

WEBB, CLIFF, et al, eds. *Haslemere, Surrey: baptisms 1595-1842; marriages 1573-1837; burials 1573-1842.* 2 fiche in folder. West Surrey F.H.S., [199-].

Headley

Headley, Surrey: christenings 1663- 1840; burials 1663-1840. 1 fiche. West Surrey F.H.S., 1999. Not seen.

Holmwood

See Dorking

Hook

BONE, MARION, & WOODMAN, JANET. *Hook, Surrey: St. Pauls church burials 1839-1912; 1913-1990 (indexed), including monumental incriptions.* 2 fiche in folder. East Surrey F.H.S. record publication **38**. [199-]

Horne

WEBB, CLIFF, et al, eds. *Horne, Surrey: baptisms 1614-1840; burials 1614-1840.* 2 fiche in folder. West Surrey F.H.S., 1996.

Horsell

WEBB, CLIFF, et al, eds. *Horsell, Surrey: baptisms 1587-1588, 1653-1840; marriages 1587; burials, 1587-1588, 1653-1840.* 2 fiche in folder. West Surrey F.H.S., 1995.

Kew

SMITH, J. CHALLENER, & WEBB, CLIFF, eds. *Kew, Surrey: baptisms 1714-91, 1800-20, 1822-40; marriages 1714-83, 1800-37; burials 1714-85, 1800-20, 1822-40.* 1 fiche. West Surrey F.H.S., 1997.

Kingston on Thames

MESLEY, BOB, et al, eds. *Kingston upon Thames, Surrey. Part 1. Baptisms 1541-1553, 1560-1665; marriages 1543-1557, 1560-1665; burials 1542-1556, 1560-1665.* 3 fiche in folder. West Surrey F.H.S., 1999.

See also Richmond

Lambeth

See Bermondsey

Leatherhead

PURKISS, JEAN, & WEBB, CLIFF, eds. *Leatherhead, Surrey: baptisms 1623, 1626, 1647, 1649, 1656-1840; burials 1656-1840.* 2 fiche in folder. West Surrey F.H.S., 1999.

CLARE, JOHN G. 'Leatherhead marriage licences 1849-1947', *E.Sy.F.H.S.J.* **17**(4), 1994, 41-2. List.

Lingfield

LEVESON-GOWER, GRANVILLE. *Extracts from the parish registers of Lingfield, Surrey.* Mitchell and Hughes, 1894. Reprinted from *M.G.H.* Baptisms 1559-1800; marriages 1576-1746; burials 1561-1810.

LEVESON-GOWER, GRANVILLE. 'Extracts from the parish registers of Lingfield, Surrey', *M.G.H.* 3rd series, **1**, 1896, 34-40 & 71-5. 16-18th c. Includes list of curates, 1675-1849.

Little Bookham

WEBB, CLIFF, et al, eds. *Little Bookham, Surrey: baptisms 1587, 1642-1840; marriages, 1670-1835; burials, 1587/88, 1642-1869.* 1 fiche in folder. West Surrey F.H.S., 1995.

DALTON, R.F. 'Little Bookham parish registers', *P.L.D.L.H.S.* 1(1), 1947, 16. Brief note.

Long Ditton

WEBB, CLIFF, & MESLEY, BOB. *Long Ditton, Surrey: baptisms 1564-1840; marriages 1564-1837; burials 1566-1858.* 2 fiche in folder. West Surrey F.H.S., 1998.

Malden

WEBB, CLIFF, ed. *Malden, Surrey: baptisms 1677-1840; marriages 1676-1837; burials 1678-1840.* 1 fiche in folder. West Surrey F.H.S., 1996.

Merrow

WEBB, CLIFF, et al, eds. *Merrow, Surrey: baptisms 1537-1840; burials 1536-1865.* 1 fiche in folder. West Surrey F.H.S., 1995.

Merrow, Surrey: registers of baptism, marriage, and burial, 1754-1812. 1 fiche in folder. East Surrey F.H.S. record publication 36. [199-]

Merstham

WOODHOUSE, REGINALD ILLINGWORTH, et al, eds. *The registers of Merstham, Surrey, 1538-1812.* Parish Register Society 42. 1902. Also issued as Surrey P.R.S. Extra volume 1.

Mickleham

SYKES, AUDREY, WEBB, CLIFF, et al, eds. *Mickleham, Surrey: baptisms 1549-1840; marriages 1549-1713; burials 1549-1840.* 1 fiche in folder. West Surrey F.H.S., 1999.

Mitcham

RICE, ROBERT GARRAWAY. 'On the parish registers of Ss. Peter and Paul, Mitcham, Surrey (from A.D.1563 to 1679)', *Reliquary* **18**, 1877-8, 1-12 & 136-44; **19**, 1878-9, 17-23 & 231-6; **20**, 1879-80, 44-8. Not completed; to 1597 only. Includes many biographical notes.

The church of St. Peter & St. Paul, Mitcham, Surrey, Dioceses of Southwark. Baptisms 1779-1812. 3 fiche in folder. East Surrey F.H.S. record publication 48. [199-.]

The church of St. Peter & St. Paul, Mitcham, Surrey, Diocese of Southwark. Burials 1779-1812. East Surrey F.H.S. record publication 49. [199-].

GALLAGHER, SHEILA. 'Mitcham St. Peter & St. Paul parish church: burial registers 1779-1812. Part I: accidental deaths', *E.Sy.F.H.S.J.* **18**(2), 1995, 12-14. Not continued.

St. Peter & St. Paul (Mitcham parish church) Mitcham, Surrey, Diocese of Southwark. Burials 1813-1833. 1 fiche in folder. East Surrey F.H.S. record publication **56**. [199-.]

St. Peter & St. Paul (Mitcham parish church) Mitcham, Surrey, Diocese of Southwark. Burials 1834-1855. 1 fiche in folder. East Surrey F.H.S. record publication **57**. [199-.]

St. Peter & St. Paul (Mitcham parish church). Mitcham, Surrey, Diocese of Southwark. Burials 1855-1884. 2 fiche in folder. East Surrey F.H.S. record publication **58**. [199-.]

Morden

CLAYTON, F., ed. *The parish registers of Morden, Co.Surrey, 1634-1812.* Surrey P.R.S. **10**. 1812. Bound with the register of Beddington. Also issued as Parish Register Society 37.

WEBB, CLIFF, ed. *Morden, Surrey: baptisms 1634-1840; marriages, 1634-1812; burials 1634-1840; and baptisms and burials 1813-1840.* 2 fiche in folder. West Surrey F.H.S., 1995.

RICE, ROBERT GARRAWAY. 'Extracts from the parish registers of Morden, Co.Surrey', *Genealogist* **7**, 1883, 33-40.

Mortlake

COCKING, MAURICE S., & GOULD, DAVID, eds. *Mortlake parish register (1599-1678).* Barnes: Borough of Barnes History Society, 1958. Duplicated typescript.

WEBB, CLIFF, et al, eds. *Mortlake, Surrey: baptisms 1677-1840; burials 1677-1840.* 3 fiche in folder. West Surrey F.H.S., 1998.

Newdigate

WEBB, CLIFF, et al, eds. *Newdigate, Surrey: baptisms 1560-1840; burials 1559-1840.* 2 fiche in folder. West Surrey F.H.S., 1999.

Nutfield

WEBB, CLIFF, & BROWN, OSSIE, et al, eds. *Nutfield, Surrey: baptisms 1557-1840; marriages 1558-1688; burials 1558-1840.* 2 fiche in folder. West Surrey F.H.S., 1999.

Oakwood

See Abinger

Ockham

WEBB, CLIFF, et al, eds. *Ockham, Surrey: baptisms 1568-1840; marriages 1568-1840; burials 1568-1840.* 2 fiche in folder. West Surrey F.H.S., 1995.

Ockley

BAX, ALFRED RIDLEY. 'The church registers and parish account books of Ockley, Co.Surrey', *Sy.A.C.* **10**, 1891, 20-78. Extracts, 16-19th c., rather than full transcripts.

WEBB, CLIFF, et al, eds. *Ockley, Surrey: baptisms, 1539-1840; marriages 1539-1599; burials, 1539-1840.* 2 fiche. West Surrey F.H.S., [199-?]

Oxted

WEBB, CLIFF, et al, eds. *Oxted, Surrey: baptisms 1613-1840; burials 1603-1840.* 2 fiche in folder. West Surrey F.H.S. 1996.

Peper Harrow

WEBB, CLIFF, et al, eds. *Peper Harrow, Surrey: baptisms, 1588, 1692-1693, 1697-1840; marriages, 1689-1690, 1692-1693; burials 1587, 1689, 1693, 1698-1840.* 1 fiche in folder. West Surrey F.H.S., 1995.

Petersham

Petersham, Surrey: baptisms 1570-1840; burials 1577-1840. 1 fiche in folder. West Surrey F.H.S., 1995. Not seen.
See also Richmond

Pirbright

SYKES, AUDREY, & WEBB, CLIFF, eds. *Pirbright, Surrey: baptisms 1574-1840; burials 1574-1840.* 2 fiche in folder. West Surrey F.H.S., 1995.

Putney

BANNERMAN, W. BRUCE, ed. *The parish register of Putney, in the County of Surrey.* 3 vols. Surrey P.R.S. **11-13**. 1913-16. 1620-1870.

COTTRELL, ROBERT J. ed. *St. Mary's, Putney: baptisms, marriages and burials, 1799-1812.* 1 fiche in folder. Thames Riverside parish index **24**. Bexleyheath: R. J. Cottrell, 1996.

WEBB, CLIFF, ed. *Putney, Surrey: baptisms and burials, 1813-1832, 1834-1837 and extracts 1833, 1838-1850.* 2 fiche in folder. West Surrey F.H.S., 1995.

Pyrford

ANDERSON, AUDREY, & WEBB, CLIFF, et al, eds. *Pyrford, Surrey: baptisms, 1587, 1665-1876; burials, 1587, 1665-1909.* 1 fiche in folder. West Surrey F.H.S., 1995.

Reigate

WEBB, CLIFF. 'Reigate Quaker register', *R. & B.* **19**(1), 1992, 15-16. See also **19**(3), 1992, 104-6. 17th c. register of baptisms, marriages and burials.

Richmond

SMITH, J. CHALLENOR, ed. *The parish registers of Richmond, Surrey.* 2 vols. Surrey P.R.S. **1 & 3**. 1903-5. 1583-1780.

HART, WILLIAM HENRY. 'Notes from the parish registers of Richmond, Kingston, and Petersham, in the County of Surrey', *Sy.A.C.* **2**, 1864, 82-98. Brief extracts.

DOLAN, AGNES, & HANSOM, JOSEPH S., eds. 'Catholic registers of St. Elizabeth's church, Richmond, Surrey', in *Miscellanea VI: Bedingfield papers.* Catholic Record Society **7**. 1909, 296-318. 1797-1839.

Rotherhithe

COTTRELL, ROBERT J., ed. *St. Mary's, Rotherhithe, Surrey: 1834-1870 baptisms and marriages; 1834-1855 burials. Excludes 1st January 1865 to 31st March 1867.* 6 fiche in folder. Thames Riverside parish index **26**. Bexleyheath: R.J.Cottrell, 1997.

St. Martha on the Hill

MESLEY, BOB, & WEBB, CLIFF, eds. *St. Martha's, Surrey: baptisms 1779-1900; burials, 1780-1900.* 1 fiche in folder. West Surrey F.H.S., 1995.

HALL, JUNE. 'Marriage licences issued at St.Martha-on-the-Hill, 1728-1742', *R. & B.* **13**(3), 1986, 92-3.

Sanderstead

BANNERMAN, W. BRUCE. ed. *The parish registers of Sanderstead, Co.Surrey.* Surrey P.R.S. **6**. 1908. Bound with the register for Gatton. 1565-1812. Reprinted in:

WEBB, CLIFF, et al, eds. *Sanderstead, Surrey: baptisms 1565-1840; marriages 1567-1835; burials 1567-1840; printed volume, 1565-1812, 1813-1840.* 1 fiche in folder. West Surrey F.H.S., 1999.

Shalford

WEBB, CLIFF, et al, eds. *Shalford, Surrey: baptisms 1564-1841; burials 1558-1841.* 1 fiche in folder. West Surrey F.H.S., 1999.
'Shalford, marriages 1567-1651', *R. & B.* **11**(1), 1984, 20-23.

Shere

Shere, Surrey: Christenings, 1547-1840; marriages, 1547-1837; burials 1546-1840. 2 fiche in folder. West Surrey F.H.S., 2000. Not seen.
HUDSON, W. 'Transcript of names in the earliest register of Shere from 1547 to 1603', *M.G.H.* 5th series, **2**, 1916-17, 166-8, 211-14, 260-68 & 306-14.

Southwark

PRUYN, JOHN V.L. 'Weddings at St. Saviour's Southwark, from A.D. 1606 to 1625', *Genealogist* N.S., **6**, 1890, 145-53 & 228-36; **7**, 1891, 26-34, 92-100, 166-73 & 233-6; **8**, 1892, 119-27; **9**, 1893, 87-92, 172-6 & 232-9.
BOVETT, ELSIE. 'Southwark strays from a Somerset nonconformist register', *R. & B.* **18**(1), 1991, 5-6. From a Taunton register, 1747-91.
See also Bermondsey

Stoke D'Abernon

BANNERMAN, W. BRUCE. ed. *The parish registers of Stoke D'Abernon, Co.Surrey.* Parish Register Society **77**. 1917. Also issued as Surrey P.R.S. **9**. 1915. In the latter volume, the register for Haslemere is also included. Reprinted in:

WEBB, CLIFF, et al, eds. *Stoke Dabernon, Surrey: baptisms 1619-1840; marriages 1621-1835; burials 1619-1840.* 1 fiche in folder. West Surrey F.H.S., [199-.]

Stoke next Guildford

WEBB, CLIFF, et al, eds. *Stoke next Guildford, Surrey: baptisms 1662-1840; burials 1662-1840.* 1 fiche in folder. West Surrey F.H.S., 1999.

Streatham

BROWN, JOHN W. 'Brief entries in the Streatham parish registers', *Local history magazine* **53**, 1996, 18. Discussion; no extracts.
BROWN, JOHN W. *The dead centre of Streatham: St. Leonard's churchyard.* Streatham: Local History Reprints, 1990. With notes on some memorials.
BROWN, JOHN W. 'St. Leonard's church: register', *E.Sy.F.H.S.J.* **17**(2), 1994, 17-19. At Streatham; general discussion with brief extracts.
N., J.G. 'Extracts from the parish register of Streatham, Co.Surrey', *Collectanea topographica et genealogica* **3**, 1836, 309-13.

Sutton

BANNERMAN, W. BRUCE. ed. *The parish registers of Sutton, Co.Surrey, 1636-1837.* Parish Register Society **74**. 1915. Also issued as Surrey P.R.S. Extra volume **2**. Reprinted with additions in:

WEBB, CLIFF. ed. *Sutton, Surrey: baptisms 1636-1851; marriages 1637-1837; burials 1631-1851.* 2 fiche in folder. West Surrey F.H.S., 1999.

Tandridge

WEBB, CLIFF, et al, eds. *Tandridge, Surrey: baptisms, 1666-1840; burials, 1695-1840.* 1 fiche in folder. West Surrey F.H.S., 1999.

Tatsfield

BANNERMAN, W. BRUCE. ed. *The parish registers of Tatsfield, Co.Surrey.* Surrey P.R.S. **4**. 1906. 1689-1812. Bound with the registers of Farleigh and Wanborough.

Thames Ditton

WEBB, CLIFF, et al, eds. *Thames Ditton, Surrey: baptisms 1663-1689, 1692-1693, 1701, 1752-1840; marriages 1663-1694, 1701; burials 1663-1694, 1701, 1763-1840.* 2 fiche in folder. West Surrey F.H.S., 1996.

Titsey

BANNERMAN, W. BRUCE, ed. *The parish registers of Titsey, Co.Surrey.* Surrey P.R.S. **7.** 1909. 1579-1812. Bound with the register for Chipstead. Reprinted on fiche, with additions 1813-40, West Surrey F.H.S., 1999.

Virginia Water

See Egham

Walton on Thames

SYKES, AUDREY, WEBB, CLIFF, et al, eds. *Walton on Thames, Surrey: baptisms 1639-1840; burials 1639-1840.* 2 fiche in folder. West Surrey F.H.S., 1999.

Walton on the Hill

MESLEY, BOB, WEBB, CLIFF. et al, eds. *Walton on the Hill, Surrey: baptisms 1581-1840; burials 1631-1840.* 1 fiche in folder. West Surrey F.H.S., 1999.

MARSHALL, GEORGE W. 'Church notes from Walton-on-the-Hill, Co.Surrey', *Reliquary* **10,** 1869-70, 203-5. Includes extracts from parish registers and monumental inscriptions.

Wanborough

PALMER, P.G., & BANNERMAN, W. BRUCE, eds. *The parish register book of Wanborough, Co. Surrey.* Surrey P.R.S. **4.** 1906. 1561-1675. Brief. Bound with the registers of Farleigh, Tatfield and Woldingham. Reprinted on 1 fiche (in folder). West Surrey F.H.S., [1995.]

Wandsworth

SQUIRE, JOHN TRAVISS, ed. *The registers of the parish of Wandsworth in the County of Surrey (1603-1787).* Lymington: Chas. T. King, 1889.

DAVIS, CECIL T. 'Marriages of Wandsworth inhabitants', *M.G.H.* 3rd series, **3,** 1900, 195-7, 231-5 & 278-85; 3rd series, **4,** 1902, 12-15, 38-41, 89-92, 143-7, 170-74, 202-4, 233-6 & 281-3; 3rd series **5,** 1904, 28-33, 74-8, 90-95 & 138-43; 4th series **3,** 1910, 145-50. Marriages in various churches in London and Surrey, *etc.,* of Wandsworth inhabitants, including notes on related baptisms and burials.

'Marriages of Wandsworth people not solemnized in the parish church, and, marriage allegations of Wandsworth people whether solemnized at Wandsworth or not, 1584-1687', *Wandsworth notes and queries* **12,** 1899, 229-42.

DAVIS, CECIL T. 'Burials at Wandsworth, 1678, October 29, to 1727, April 4', *Sy.A.C.* **14,** 1899, 134-63. Extracts from the churchwardens' account book relating to funerals.

See also Bermondsey

Warlingham

BANNERMAN, W. BRUCE, ed. *The parish registers of Warlingham, Co.Surrey.* Surrey P.R.S. **5.** Bound with the registers of Addington and Chelsham. Reprinted on 1 fiche, with addition of 1813-40, West Surrey F.H.S., 1999.

West Clandon

SYKES, AUDREY, & WEBB, CLIFF. et al, eds. *West Clandon, Surrey: baptisms 1536-1840; burials, 1536-1840.* 2 fiche in folder. West Surrey F.H.S., 1995.

West Horsley

WEBB, CLIFF, et al, eds. *West Horsley, Surrey: baptisms 1606-1840; burials 1600-1840.* 1 fiche in folder. West Surrey F.H.S., 1998.

West Molesey

WEBB, CLIFF, et al, eds. *West Molesey, Surrey: baptisms 1729-1840; marriages, 1729-1837; burials, 1729-1840.* 1 fiche in folder. West Surrey F.H.S., 1996.

Weybridge

LLOYD, ELEANOR. 'Weybridge parish registers', *Sy.A.C.* **17,** 1902, 41-69. General discussion with some extracts. Not a transcript.

See also Woburn

Wimbledon

CLARKE, A.W.HUGHES, ed. *The parish register of Wimbledon, Co.Surrey.* Mitchell, Hughes & Clarke for the John Evelyn Club for Wimbledon, 1924. Also issued as Sy.R.S. **8**. 1925. (No. **22** of the Society's publications). 1538-1812. Reprinted with additions in:

WEBB, CLIFF, et al, eds. *Wimbledon, Surrey: baptisms 1538-1812; marriages 1594-1812; burials 1588-1812, from the printed edition of 1924. Baptisms 1813-1840; burials 1813-1840.* 3 fiche in folder. West Surrey F.H.S., 1999.

Windlesham

GLANVILLE-RICHARDS, WILLIAM URMSTON SEARLE, ed. *The registers of Windlesham, Surrey, from 1677 to 1783, with biographical notices of some past and present families now residing in the parish, etc.* Mitchell and Hughes, 1881. Reprinted with additions in:

WEBB, CLIFF, ed. *Windlesham, Surrey: baptisms 1677-1698, 1717-1899; marriages 1695-1696, 1717-1899; burials, 1695-1698, 1717-1865, and Bagshot, Surrey: baptisms, 1837-1840; burials 1837-1841.* 4 fiche in folder. West Surrey F.H.S., 1996.

Wisley

SYKES, AUDREY. & WEBB, CLIFF, et al, eds. *Wisley, Surrey: baptisms 1667-1901; marriages 1837-1901; burials 1657-1901.* 1 fiche in folder. West Surrey F.H.S., 1995.

Witley

WEBB, CLIFF, et al, eds. *Witley, Surrey: baptisms, 1653-1840; burials 1653-1840.* 3 fiche in folder. West Surrey F.H.S., 1995.

Woburn Lodge

CRISP, FREDERICK ARTHUR, ed. *Catholic registers of Woburn-Lodge Chapel and Weybridge, Surrey.* [ ]: F.A.Crisp, 1888. 1750-1874.

Woldingham

RICE, R. GARRAWAY, ed. *The parish register book of Woldingham, Co.Surrey, 1765 to 1812.* Surrey P.R.S. **4**. 1906. Bound with the registers of Farleigh, Tatfield and Wanborough. Brief.

Woldingham, Surrey: christenings 1765-1840; marriages 1765-1837; burials 1765-1865. 1 fiche. West Surrey F.H.S., 1999. Not seen.

Wonersh

HENDERSON, ROSEMARY, et al, eds. *Wonersh, Surrey: baptisms 1539-1841; burials 1539-1841.* 2 fiche in folder. West Surrey F.H.S., 1999.

Woodmansterne

BUSFIELD, DONALD W. *Woodmansterne, Surrey. St. Peter's church parish registers 1566-1837.* 1 fiche. East Surrey F.H.S. record publication **17**. 1987.

Worplesdon

SYKES, AUDREY, WEBB, CLIFF, et al, eds. *Worplesdon, Surrey: baptisms 1538-1539, 1570-1840; burials 1570-1840.* 2 fiche in folder. West Surrey F.H.S., 1999.

Wotton

See Abinger

SUSSEX

Alfriston

EXCELL, PHYL, & EXCELL, STAN. 'Alfriston & its parish register', *Sx.F.H.* **5**, 1982, 14-16. Brief discussion.

Angmering

PENFOLD, EDWARD W.D., ed. *The first book of the parish registers of Angmering, Sussex, 1562-1687.* Sx.R.S. **18**. 1913.

Ardingly

LODER, GERALD W.E., ed. *The parish registers of Ardingly, Sussex, 1558-1812.* Sx.R.S. **17**. 1913.

Ashburnham

WHISTLER, ROSE FULLER. 'The Ashburnham registers', *Sx.A.C.* **33**, 1883, 49-68. General discussion, with brief extracts, list of incumbents, list of contributors, 1670, to a collection for the redemption of Turkish captives, *etc.*

Beddingham

STEVENS, F.BENTHAM. 'Registers and papers of St. Andrew's, Beddingham', *Sx.A.C.* **54**, 1911, 263-4. List of parish registers, *etc.* No extracts.

Berwick

ELLMAN, E.B. 'Family names in Berwick, from 1606-1812', *Sx.A.C.* **22**, 1870, 22-9. See also **39**, 1894, 226. Lists surnames found in the parish register.

Billinghurst

MAGUIRE, LEONARD J. *The General Baptist Meeting House now known as the Free Christian Church (Unitarian) Billingshurst: composite register of deaths and monumental inscriptions.* L. J. Maguire for the General Baptist Assembly, 1985. Register covers 1755-1980.

Bodle Street Green

WHITE, DOROTHY. *St. John's church, Bodle Street Green, Sussex: baptisms 1856-1986.* [Eastbourne]: Family Roots F.H.S., 1990.

WHITE, DOROTHY. *St. John's church, Bodle Street Green, Sussex: marriages, 1856-1986; banns 1857-1982.* [Eastbourne]: Family Roots F.H.S. (Eastbourne & District), 1990.

WHITE, DOROTHY. *St. John's church, Bodle Street Green, Sussex: burials 1856-1986, & monumental inscriptions.* [Eastbourne]: Family Roots F.H.S. (Eastbourne & District), 1990.

Bolney

HUTH, EDWARD, ed. *The parish registers of Bolney, Sussex, 1541-1812.* Sx.R.S. **15**. 1912.

Bosham

MACDERMOTT, K.H. 'Extracts from the parish registers of Bosham, Sussex', *Sx.A.C.* **54**, 1911, 55-61. Brief.

Brighton

ROBERTS, HENRY D. ed. *The parish registers of Brighton in the County of Sussex, 1558-1701.* Brighton: Corporation of Brighton, 1932.

Brighton baptisms 1813-1837. 6 fiche in folder. Microfiche series **PF11**. [ ]: Sussex Family History Group, 1993.

'East Sussex C.R.O., Lewes: parish register of St. Nicholas, Brighthelmstone [Brighton]: marriages of South Glos. militiamen', *Journal of Gloucestershire Family History Society* **40**, 1989, 26; **41**, 1989, 28. See also **42**, 1989, 11. 1800-1809.

Burchall

BURCHALL, M.J. *Brighton Presbyterian registers 1700-1837.* Brighton: Sussex Family History Group, 1979.

Clapham

GROVER, J.W. 'Notes on old Clapham registers and parish documents', *Journal of the British Archaeological Association* **41**, 1885, 299-306. Brief note, including a handful of extracts from the registers.

Cocking

CHALLEN, W.H., ed. *The parish register of Cocking, Sussex, 1558-1837.* Mitchell, Hughes and Clarke, 1927.

Cowfold

GODMAN, P.S., ed. *The parish register of Cowfold, Sussex, 1558-1812.* Sx.R.S. **22**. 1916.

Cuckfield

RENSHAW, W.C. ed. *The parish registers of Cuckfield, Sussex, 1598-1699.* Sx.R.S. **13**. 1911.

THORN, JUNE. 'Extracts from parish records of Cuckfield, Sussex', *H. & R.F.H.S.J.* **6**(4), 1992, 80-81. 17th c.

Ditchling

MAGUIRE, LEONARD J. *The registers of births, deaths and burials for the General Baptist Meeting at Ditchling, covering part of the period 1786-1837.* South Croydon: the author, 1977.

MAGUIRE, LEONARD J., *Records of the Old Meeting House, Ditchling, Sussex. Volume II. Registers and monumental inscriptions.* Ditchling: L.J.Maguire, 1978. General Baptist and Unitarian etc. Includes births, 1798-1832; deaths and burials, 1821-1950.

Darrington

'Parish register of Darrington, Sussex', *M.G.H.* 5th series, **3**, 1918-19, 23-30 & 96-104. 1626-1752.

East Blatchington

LAYTON, JOHN H., & WILLIAMS, FRANK R., eds. *The parish registers of East Blatchington, Sussex, 1563-1804.* Seaford: Frank R. Williams, 1940.

East Dean
See Singleton

East Grinstead
CRAWFURD, R.P., ed. *The parish register of East Grinstead, Sussex, 1558-1661.* Sx.R.S. **24**. 1917.
LEPPARD, M.J. 'East Grinstead's earliest parish register', *Sx.F.H.* **4**(7), 1981, 223. Brief note.
LEPPARD, M.J. 'East Grinstead's earliest parish register', *Bulletin of the East Grinstead Society* **29**, 1980, 10. Brief note.
WOOD, R.H. 'Musings on the parish registers', *Bulletin of the East Grinstead Society* **3**, 1970, 7-8. Brief extracts.

Eastbourne
Eastbourne baptisms St. Mary's parish church, Eastbourne, Sussex, 1558-1837. 5 pts. Eastbourne: PBN Publications, 1992-4.
GAUTREY, ARTHUR J. [ed.] *Eastbourne marriages: St. Mary's parish church, 1558-1753.* Eastbourne: PBN Publications, 1991.
GAUTREY, ARTHUR J., ed. *Eastbourne marriages, St. Mary's parish church, Eastbourne, 1754-1837.* Eastbourne: PBN Publications, 1993.
Eastbourne burials: St. Mary's parish church, 1558-1837. 2 fiche in folder. Eastbourne: PBN Publications, 1991.

Edburton
WILKIE, C.H., ed. *S.Andrews, Edburton, Sussex: copy of parish register book, 1558-1673.* Brighton: J.G.Bishop, 1884. Indexed in:
Index to registers of Edburton, Sussex, 1558-1673. Frederick Arthur Crisp, 1887.
WILKIE, CHRISTOPHER HALES. *St. Andrews, Edburton, Sussex: second parish register book, 1656-1812.* Brighton: J.G.Bishop, 1900. 30 copies only printed.
GODDARD, JOAN. *Parish record transcriptions and surname index for the church of St. Andrew, Edburton: baptisms, 1888-1910; marriages 1837-1910; burials 1813-1890.* 1 fiche in folder. Microfiche series PP04. [ ]: Sussex Family History Group, 1997.

Glynde
SALZMAN, L.F., ed. *The parish register of Glynde, Sussex, 1558-1812.* Sx.R.S. **30**. 1924.
CROIX, W. DE ST. 'Names from the register books of the parish of Glynde, from 1558 to 1812', *Sx.A.C.* **24**, 1872, 99-114. Alphabetical list of surnames; also names of persons from other parishes married at Glynde.

Hailsham
MEDHURST, L., & PITCHER, E. *Hailsham burial registers, 1872-1972.* Eastbourne: Family Roots F.H.S. (Eastbourne & District), 1996.
SALZMAN, L.F. *The history of the parish of Hailsham, the abbey of Otham, and the priory of Michelham.* Lewes: Farncombe & Co., 1901. Includes marriages, 1558-1600, and consents of marriages, 1653-58.

Hastings
BAINES, J. MANWARING, ed. *Hastings baptisms 1700-1877.* 6 fiche in 2 folders. Eastbourne: PBN Publications, 1995. Covers All Saints, Croft Chapel, Ore parish church, St. Clements, St. Mary in the Castle, Wesleyan Methodist chapel.
CHALLEN, FREDERICK K. *St.Mary-in-the-Castle burial services, 1828-1900*, ed. C. Swarbrooke. Hastings: Hastings & Rother F.H.S., 1995.
VAN DEN BERGH, HEATHER. 'Canterbury marriage licences', *H. & R.F.H.S.J.* **10**(1), 1995, 18-19. Extracts relating to Hastings, 16-18th c.
'And more deaths: deaths extracted from Christ Church, Blacklands, Hastings, 1893-1896', *H. & R.F.H.S.J.* **11**(4), 1996, 65-6.

Hastings Union
Hastings Union notices of marriage 1837-1865. 2 fiche in folder. Eastbourne: PBN Publications, 1995.
Hastings Union: notices of marriages, August 1815-May 1879. 3 fiche in folder. Eastbourne: PBN Publications, 1995.

Heathfield
BURGESS, DON. 'Looking behind the registers', *Sx.F.H.* **13**(5), 1999, 166-7. Discussion of Heathfield parish register.

Heene

PRESSEY, W.J. *The earliest register of Heene (1594-1751), being a register of baptisms, marriages and burials during the period when Heene was part of the parish of West Tarring.* [ ]: [The author], [c.1935].

Horley

EWING, BRIDGET. 'Stray entries from Horley, Surrey', *Sx.G.L.H.* 2(1), 1980, 38-9. From the parish register.

Horsham

RICE, R. GARRAWAY. ed. *The parish register of Horsham in the County of Sussex, 1541-1635.* Sx.R.S. 21. 1915.

MAGUIRE, LEONARD J. *Record of the Gerard Baptist Meeting House (now Unitarian), Horsham, Sussex.* 2 vols. Horsham: L.J.Maguire, 1981-2. v.1. Registers and monumental inscriptions. v.2. Trust deeds. The registers include births, 1688-1837 and deaths/burials 1748-1837.

RICE, ROBERT GARRAWAY. 'The Derbyshire Militia at Horsham, Sussex, in 1797', *Reliquary* 19, 1878-9, 128. Parish register extracts and monumental inscriptions.

Horsted Keynes

LEVESON GOWER, GRANVILLE. 'Extracts from the parish registers of Horsted Keynes, Sussex', *M.G.H.* 2nd series, 1, 1886, 193-6. Miscellaneous extracts, 17-19th c.

Hove

SALMON, ERNEST FREDK. ed. *The parish registers of Hove and Preston, 1538-1812.* Mitchell, Hughes and Clarke, 1912. Reprinted on CD, ArchiveCD Books, c.2000.

Lewes

BURCHALL, MICHAEL J. *Lewes non-conformist registers: Westgate Chapel; Independent Tabernacle; Bethesda Chapel.* [ ]: Manuscripts of Sussex, 1975. Includes Westgate births and baptisms 1742-1834, Bethesda Chapel births and baptisms 1817-42, Independent Tabernacle births and baptisms 1817-39.

BURRELL, JOAN. 'Sussex strays: - with a difference! Baptized in Sussex but recorded in Bermondsey', *Sx.F.H.* 5(6), 1983, 192-3. Baptisms at Lewes, 1781.

HENRY, M., ed. *St. Mary's Westout, Lewes: bishops transcripts 1608, 1610-2, 1616-7, 1620, 1625, 1627-33, 1636, 1672-3, 1677-8.* [ ]: Sussex Family History Group, 1996.

'Parish register of All Saints, Lewes', *Sx.N.Q.* 7, 1938-9, 222 & 246-7; 8, 1940-41, 27-8. Brief extracts, 17th c.,

'In memoriam', *Sx.F.H.* 1(1), 1973, 10. Brief extracts from the burial register of St. John sub Castro, Lewes, 1737-49.

Littlehampton

CHALLEN, W.H., ed. 'Parish registers of the church of St. Mary the Virgin, Littlehampton to 1753', in ROBINSON, EVA, & HEWARD, J.S. *Reminiscences of Littlehampton.* Natural Science and Archaeological Society (Littlehampton) extra publication 2. 1933, 36-58. Begins in 1611.

New Shoreham

'Extract from registers of New Shoreham, Sussex, commencing 1565, *Genealogist* 5, 1881, 115. 16-17th c.

Old Shoreham

'Extracts from registers of Old Shoreham, Sussex', *Genealogist* 5, 1881, 115-6.

Ore

LISTER, A. '[Extracts from Ore marriage records, 1764-1814]', *H. & R.F.H.S.J.* 11(3), 1996, 45-7. Also war memorial and list of 1894 baptisms, *etc.*

Pett

WICKING, BENNY. 'Marriages at Pett', *H. & R.F.H.S.J.* 12(1), 1997, 11-12. 1675-1752.

Petworth

LEESON, FRANK. 'Petworth's earliest parish register', *W.Sx.H.* 54, 1994, 29-30. Brief note.

WELCH, C.E. 'The earliest parish register of Petworth', *Sx.N.Q.* 15, 1958-62, 55-7. Brief discussion.

Poynings

GODDARD, JUNE. *Parish record transcriptions and surname index for the church of the Holy Trinity, Poynings: baptisms, 1813-1910; marriages 1837-1910; burials 1813-1890.* 1 fiche in folder. Microfiche series **PP01.** [ ]: Sussex Family History Group, 1997.

Preston

GRANT, ROY C. *Military baptisms, marriages & burials at the church of St. Peter, Preston Village, Brighton, Sussex (1793-1840.* [ ]: Sussex Family History Group, [199-].
See also Hove

Pyecombe

GODDARD, JOAN. *Parish record transcriptions and surname index for the church of the Transfiguration, Pyecombe: baptisms 1896-1911; marriages 1839-1911; burials 1813-1912.* 1 fiche in folder. Microfiche series **PP02.** [ ]: Sussex Family History Group, 1997.

Rogate

LEESON, F.L. 'Marriages in Rogate's earliest register', *W.Sx.H.* **56,** 1995, 25. Brief note.

Rudgwick

LEESON, FRANK. 'Rudgwick parish registers', *W.Sx.H.* **61,** 1998, 8-9. Brief note.

Rye

LISTER, A. 'Baptisms, marriages and burials from Rye parish magazines, 1894', *H.& R.F.H.S.J.* **11**(4), 1996, 64; **12**(2), 1197, 29-30.

Seaford

'Sad sagas from Seaford in Sussex', *H. & R.F.H.S.J.* **6**(1), 1991, 10. Brief extracts, 18-19th c., from the parish register.

Selham

BISHOP, JOHN H. 'Parsons & pluralities: some points from Selham registers 1565-1837', *Sx.F.H.* **4**(6), 1980, 190-91. General discussion.

BISHOP, JOHN H. 'Some points from Selham parish registers 1565 to 1837', *West Sussex Archives Society newsletter* **8,** 1977, 18-20. Brief discussion.

Singleton

'Strays and foreigners', *R. & B.* **2**(2), 1975, 43-5. Mainly from the registers of Singleton, Sussex, and East Dean.

Steyning

BREACH, W. POWELL. 'Steyning marriages, &c., during the Commonwealth, 1653 to 1658', *Sx.A.C.* **42,** 1899, 111-16.

Tarring

PRESSEY, W.J., ed. *The Tarring registers.* 3 vols. [ ]: [the editor], [c.1935.] v.1. 1540-1655. v.2. 1657-1698. v.3. 1699-1743.

Telscombe

'Marriages at Telscombe, 1612-1686', *Sx.G.L.H.* **7**(1), 1985, 23-4. From the bishops' transcripts.

Thakeham

LEESON, F.L. 'The earliest registers of Thakeham and Washington', *W.Sx.H.* **58,** 1996, 2. Brief note.

Tuxlith

RAKE, L.G.L., ed. *The Tuxlith folk book: a register of all people known to have been baptised, married, or buried at Tuxlith Chapel, Milland, and Rake, 1581-1879.* Tuxlith tracts **3.** Liss: Friends of Tuxlith Chapel, 1995.

Washington

JENNER, A. 'The first Washington parish register', *West Sussex Archives Society newsletter* **9,** 1978, 12-13. Brief note.
See also Thakeham

West Firle

NASH, E.H. 'Registers and papers of St. Peter's, West Firle', *Sx.A.C.* **54,** 1911, 263. List of registers; no extracts.

West Tarring
See also Heene

Willingdon

BERRY, H. 'Willingdon parish church: review of the first registers', *E.L.H.S.N.* **16,** 1975, 2-5. General discussion.

GAUTREY, ARTHUR J. 'Military marriages at Willingdon in Napoleonic times', *E.L.H.S.N.* **13**, 1974, 5-6. See also **14**, 1975, 4. Extracts from the parish registers.

Winchelsea
LEESON, FRANK. 'Winchelsea, Sx., 1655-7', *Sx.F.H.* **12**(6), 1997, 220. Brief note of marriages not found in the parish register.

Withyham
LEPPARD, M.J. 'Withyham marriages, and others', *Sx.F.H.* **5**(6), 1983, 194. Brief note on the register.

Woodmancote
SYKES-MACLEAN, HECTOR, ed. *The registers of the parish of Woodmancote in the County of Sussex: baptisms, burials and marriages 1582-1812.* Brighton: Southern Publishing, 1932. Includes lists of rectors, churchwardens, waywardens, and overseers.

2. MONUMENTAL INSCRIPTIONS

Monumental inscriptions frequently provide information additional to that found in parish registers, and are a valuable source of genealogical information, especially for recent centuries. Many have been transcribed; the majority of transcripts have not, however, been published. For lists of transcripts (now somewhat dated) see:

WILCOCK, TIM. *The monumental inscriptions of Surrey, a list of copies.* 2nd ed. West Surrey F.H.S research aids **19**. 1991.

EXCEL, PHYL., & EXCEL, STANLEY. 'Monumental transcriptions in the library of the Sussex Archaeological Society', *Sx.F.H.* **4**(2), 1979, 47-8.

LEESON, FRANK. 'West Sussex M.I's', *Sx.F.H.* **4**(2), 1979, 69-72; **4**(3), 1980, 108. List of all known transcripts

For a list of crematoria in Surrey, see:

BLAKE, PAUL. 'Surrey crematoria', *E.Sy.F.H.S.J.* **16**(2), 1993, 19 A0. List of all Surrey crematoria.

Cemeteries and crematoria in Metropolitan Surrey are listed in:

WEBB, CLIFF. *Greater London cemeteries and crematoria.* 6th ed. Society of Genealogists, 1999.

General works on inscriptions include:

LAMBERT, HENRY, SIR. 'The older Surrey epitaphs', *Sy.A.C.* **43**, 1935, 36-48. General discussion.

ARSCOTT, DAVID. *Dead and buried in Sussex.* Seaford: S.B.Publications, 1997. Cover: 'A unique guide to the county's strange, striking and humourous epitaphs & memorials'.

War Memorials
BILBROUGH, PETER J. *First World War graves in Sussex.* [ ]: West Sussex Family History Group, 1992.

BILBROUGH, PETER J. *Second World War graves in Sussex.* [ ]: Sussex Family History Group, 1993.

MEDHURST, L. & PITCHER, E. *Rolls of honour and war memorials in some East Sussex villages.* 8 vols. [ ]: Family Roots F.H.S. (Eastbourne & District), 1991-4. Later vols. also include 'some border villages of Kent and Surrey'.

Surrey war memorials index. 4 fiche in folder. West Surrey F.H.S. microfiche series **28**. 2000.

Brasses

STEPHENSON, MILL. *A list of monumental brasses in Surrey.* Originally reprinted from *Sy.A.C.* 1921. Reprinted Bath: Kingsmead Reprints, 1970.

STEPHENSON, MILL. 'A list of monumental brasses in Surrey', *Sy.A.C.* **25**, 1912, 33-100; **26**, 1913, 1-80; **27**, 1914, 21-87; **28**, 1915, 51-110; **29**, 1916, 79-139; **30**, 1917, 61-104; **31**, 1918, 85-128; **32**, 1919, 63-130; **33**, 1920, 1-72. See also **40**, 1932, 107-16.

STEPHENSON, M. 'List of monumental brasses in Surrey', *Transactions of the Monumental Brass Society* **6**, 1910-14, 257-318, 329-71 & 377-420.

STEPHENSON, MILL. 'Monumental brasses in Surrey', *Transactions of the St. Pauls Ecclesiological Society* **3**, 1895, 186-94.

STEPHENSON, MILL. 'Palimpsest brasses in Surrey', *Sy.A.C.* **15**, 1900, 27-39. See also **17**, 1902, 181; **18**, 1903, 219-20.

BLATCHLY, JOHN M. 'Further notes on the monumental brasses of Surrey, and the collection of rubbings at Castle Arch', *Sy.A.C.* **68**, 1971, 31-8.

BOULTER-COOKE, M. ADELINE. 'Sussex monumental brasses', *Sussex county magazine* **2**, 1928, 306-11. Brief discussion.

DAVIDSON-HOUSTON, C.E.D., MRS. 'Sussex monumental brasses', *Sx.A.C.* **76**, 1935, 46-114; **77**, 1936, 130-94; **78**, 1937, 63-125; **79**, 1938, 74-130; **80**, 1939, 93-148. See also **86**, 1947, 118-25.

WOODMAN, T.C. *The Sussex brasses.* 2 pts. Hove: Emery & Son, 1903.

TURNER, EDWARD. 'Brasses in Sussex churches', *Sx.A.C.* **23**, 1871, 129-91.

SHOOSMITH, ERNEST. 'Medieval church brasses in Sussex', *Sussex county magazine* **22**, 1948, 96-8. Brief note.

WAREING, T. 'Notes on a brass rubbing tour in West Sussex', *Monumental Brass Society transactions* **17**, 1926, 295-300; **18**, 1927, 332-7.

Hatchments

SUMMERS, PETER, & TITTERTON, JOHN, eds. *Hatchments in Britain 5: Kent, Surrey and Sussex.* Phillimore & Co., 1985.

Indents

SADLER, A.G. *The indents of lost monumental brasses in southern England.* Ferring on Sea: the author, 1976. There are 4 appendices separately published.

SADLER, A.G. *The indents of lost monumental brasses in Surrey and East Sussex.* Ferring on Sea: the author, 1975. Separately published appendix, 1980.

SADLER, A.G. *The indents of lost monumental brasses in West Sussex.* Ferring on Sea: the author, 1975.

SADLER, A.G. *The lost monumental brasses of East Sussex.* Ferring on Sea: the author, 1970.

SADLER, A.G. *The lost monumental brasses of Sussex.* Ferring on Sea; the author, 1988.

SADLER, A.G. *The lost monumental brasses of West Sussex.* [ ]: the author, 1969.

Iron Graveslabs

WILLATS, ROSALIND M. 'Pre-industrial revolution cast iron graveslabs', *Wealden iron: bulletin of the Wealden Iron Research Group* 2nd series, **8**, 1988, 12-47. Mainly Sussex, but also in Kent and Surrey, *etc.* Also published on fiche in *Sx.A.C.* **125**, 1987.

Effigies

MOSSE, H.R. *The monumental effigies of Sussex, (1250-1650).* 2nd ed. Hove: Combridges, 1933.

Memorials by Particular Masons

GUNNIS, RUPERT. 'Monuments by John Flaxman in Sussex', *Sx.A.C.* **97**, 1959, 82-8. The focus is on church monuments as sculptures, but also includes a few notes on inscriptions.

REMNANT, G.L. 'Jonathan Harmer's terracottas', *Sx.A.C.* **100**, 1962, 142-8. See also **102**, 1964, 52-5. Includes notes on memorials by this stone-mason, with notes on inscriptions; also notes on the Harmer family, with pedigree, 18-19th c.

Church Heraldry

POINTER, H.W. 'Coats of arms in Surrey churches', *Sy.A.C.* **48**, 1943, 61-112; **50**, 1949, 105-32; **52**, 1952, 69-79; **55**, 1958, 32-40; **61**, 1964, 39-50. See also **49**, 1946, 130; **52**, 1902, 66-8. Includes a few pedigrees.

LAMBARDE, FANE. 'Coats of arms in Sussex churches', *Sx.A.C.* **67**, 1926, 149-87; **68**, 1927, 210-37; **69**, 128, 190-221; **70**, 1929, 134-64; **71**, 1930, 135-70; **72**, 1931, 218-42; **73**, 1932, 102-44; **74**, 1933, 181-208; **75**, 1934, 171-89.

Monumental Strays

NEWMAN, RONALD F. 'Monuments of Sussex interest in Kentish churches: Benenden', *Sx.N.Q.* **17**, 1968-71, 137-8.

NEWMAN, RONALD F. 'Monuments of Surrey interest in Kentish churches: Benenden', *Sy.A.C.* **66**, 1969, 130. Commemorating Charles Marshall of Ripley Court, and Daniel Boys, whose wife was a member of the Richardson family of Bermondsey.

NEWMAN, RONALD F. 'Monuments of Surrey interest in Kentish churches: Chiddingstone', *Sy.A.C.* **66**, 1969, 130. Commemorating members of the Streatfield family of Wandsworth and Long Ditton, 1768 and 1809.

NEWMAN, RONALD F. 'Further monuments of Sussex interest in Kentish churches', *Sx.N.Q.* **17**, 1968-71, 152-5. At Chislet, Smarden, and Hawkhurst.

NEWMAN, RONALD F. 'Monuments of Surrey interest in Kentish churches', *Sy.A.C.* **70**, 1974, 167-9. Notes on various monuments at Lydd and Tenterden.

SURREY

Abinger

WEBB, CLIFF. 'Further pre 1866 M.I', *R. & B.* **12**(4), 1986, 148-9. Surnames only for Abinger, Mickleham, Oakwood, Ockley, Reigate, Stoke D'Abernon, Westcott and Wotton.

Addington

St. Mary the Blessed Virgin, Addington, Surrey: memorial inscriptions, 1216-1994. 3 fiche in folder. East Surrey F.H.S. record publication **M70**. [199-.]
See also Croydon

Addlestone

'Memorial inscriptions from Addlestone closed churchyard, by St. Paul's Church, Addlestone, Weybridge, Surrey', *R. & B.* **1**(1), 1974, 13-16; **1**(2), 1974, 57-60; **1**(3), 1975, 94-7. See also **2**(1), 1975, 38.

Ash

North West Surrey (Ash, Chobham, Frimley, Horsell, Pirbright, Thorpe, Windlesham). 1 fiche in folder. Monumental inscriptions on microfiche **3**. West Surrey F.H.S., 1990.

Beddington

Monumental inscriptions of the parish church of St. Mary the Virgin, Beddington, Sutton, Surrey, 1294-1997. 2 fiche in folder. East Surrey F.H.S. record publication **M73**. 1999.
See also Croydon

Benhilton

All Saints Church, Benhilton, Sutton, Surrey: recordings of monumental inscriptions, 1837-1992. 2 fiche in folder. East Surrey F.H.S. record publication **50**. [1993?]

Bisley

See Wisley

Bramley

DOWNHAM, JUNE. 'Holy Trinity, Bramley: monumental inscriptions and plaques', *R. & B.* **17**(1), 1990, 4-6.
See also Shalford

Brookwood

CLARKE, JOHN. *An introduction to Brookwood Cemetery.* Brookwood: Necropolis Publications, 1991. Includes brief descriptions of 62 headstones.

CLARKE, JOHN M. *The Brookwood Necropolis Railway.* 3rd ed. Oxford: Oakwood Press for Brookwood Cemetery Society, 1995. Study of a unique service for funerals.

Necropolis news: a six monthly magazine about Brookwood Cemetery. Woking: Brookwood Cemetery Society, 1993- . First issue only seen.

Bugby

See Epsom

Byfleet

WEBB, CLIFF. 'Byfleet memorial insriptions', *R. & B.* **6**(1), 1979, 23-30.

East of Guildford (Byfleet, Clandons, Horsleys, Merrow, Old Woking). 1 fiche in folder. Monumental inscriptions on microfiche **4**. West Surrey F.H.S., 1990.

Camberwell

CRISP, F.A. 'List of some of the graves at St. Giles, Camberwell, Co.Surrey', *Fragmenta genealogica* **6**, 1901, 17-18.

JOHNSTON, PHILIP MAINWARING. 'Old Camberwell', *Transactions of the London and Middlesex Archaeological Society* N.S., **3**, 1917, 123-184 & 217-54. Includes many monumental inscriptions from St. Giles.

S[TEINMAN], G.S. 'Some account of the arms and other paintings now or formerly in the windows of the church of St. Giles, Camberwell', *Collectanea topographica et genealogica* **2**, 1935, 114-9.

Carshalton

S[TEINMAN], G.S. 'Epitaphs, persons and arms formerly in Carshalton church, Surrey', *Collectanea topographica et genealogica* **3**, 1836, 327-9.

WALLER, J.G. 'On the monuments in Carshalton church, Surrey', *Sy.A.C.* **7**, 1880, 67-76.

Caterham

BURGESS, FREDERICK. 'Local churchyard monuments', *L.H.R.* **6**, 1967, 26-31. Brief notes on inscriptions in the Caterham area.

Chaldon

Monumental inscriptions, 1656-1987: the church of St. Peter and St. Paul, Chaldon, Surrey. 1 fiche. East Surrey F.H.S. record publication **20**. 1988.

Charlwood

ANDRÉ, J. LEWIS. 'Charlwood church', *Sy.A.C.* **11**, 1893, 1-24. Includes inscriptions in the church.

Cheam

KING, WILLIAM WARWICK. 'Monumental memoranda from Cheam church', *Sy.A.C.* **3**, 1865, 324-48. Primarily relating to the Lumley monument, and its various brasses.

Cheam Common

Cheam Common, Surrey. St. Philip's church, monumental inscriptions, 1881-1983. 2 fiche. East Surrey F.H.S. record publication **15**. 1987.

Chelsham

Chelsham, St. Leonard, Surrey: monumental inscriptions 1250-1988. 1 fiche. East Surrey F.H.S. record publication **30**. 1990.

Chiddingfold

See Godalming

Chipstead

Chipstead St. Margaret, Surrey. Monumental inscriptions 1303-1989. 3 fiche. East Surrey F.H.S. record publication **32**. 1990.

Chobham

See Ash

Clandons

See Byfleet

Clapham

DALE, T.C. *Our Clapham forefathers, being a list of inscriptions from the tombs, monuments and head-stones of the old parish churchyard, with notes and an index of names.* [Clapham Observer], [1921].

Claygate

HENDERSON, JULIAN, & MAIN, JOHN. 'Building for growth: the proper treatment of graves', *R. & B.* **22**(4), 1996, 136-9. Lists gravestones to be relocated or removed at Claygate.

Compton

ANDRE, J. LEWIS. 'Compton church', *Sy.A.C.* **12**, 1895, 1-19. Includes some inscriptions.

West of Guildford: (Compton, Peper Harow, Tilford, Wanborough, & Worplesdon). 1 fiche in folder. Monumental inscriptions on microfiche **6**. West Surrey F.H.S., 1990.

Crowhurst

FRENCH, GEORGE RUSSELL. 'A brief account of Crowhurst church, Surrey, and its monuments', *Sy.A.C.* **3**, 1865, 39-62.

Crowhurst, Surrey: church of St. George, monumental inscriptions. 1 fiche in folder. East Surrey F.H.S. record publication **42**. [199-].

Croydon

ANDERSON, JOHN CORBET. *Monuments and antiquities of Croydon church, in the County of Surrey, comprising a description of that structure, its monuments and brasses ...* Croydon: the author, 1856.

COX, RONALD. *At the going down of the sun ... an account of Croydon's war memorials.* The author, 1992. Includes a list - but few names of the fallen.

S[TEINMAN], G.S., 'Epitaphs formerly in Croydon church; and further extracts from te parish register of Croydon', *Collectanea topographica et genealogica* **5**, 1838, 40-44.

Croydon in the past; historical, monumental and biographical, being a history of the town as depicted on the tombs, tablets and gravestones in the churches, churchyards and cemetery of the parish, including also memorials of the neighbouring villages of Beddington, Shirley and Addington, preceded by original and interesting historical notes. Croydon: Jesse W. Ward, 1883. Reprinted as:

Croydon in the past, including monumental inscriptions of Croydon churches of St. John, St. James, St. Peter and Christ Church; Friends Meeting House and Pump Pail Chapel, Croydon; churches at Beddington, Addington and Shirley. 3 fiche in folder. East Surrey F.H.S. record publication **35**. 1992.

Deptford

PARRY, GILBERT S. 'Inscriptions in the churchyard of St. Nicholas, Deptford', *Notes & queries* 12th series **9**, 1921, 3-4 & 22-4.

Dorking

ASHCOMBE, LORD. 'Mural monuments in Dorking church', *Sy.A.C.* **12**, 1895, 20-24. 'Pre-1865 M.I's at Dorking', *R. & B.* **12**(1), 1985, 19-20. Surnames only.

Dunsfold
See Godalming

Duxbury

BROWN, A.O. 'Monumental inscriptions at Lady Somerset Homes, Duxhurst', *E.Sy.F.H.S.J.* **19**(4), 1996, 44.

Duxhurst

BROWN, OSMUND. 'Memorial inscriptions: Lady Henry Somerset Homes, Duxhurst', *R. & B.* **8**(1), 1981, 26-7. 20th c.

East Horsley

WARD, O.I. 'Exeter memories in Surrey', *Devon & Cornwall notes & queries* **18**, 1934, 60-62. 13th c. brasses at East Horsley.

Elstead
See Thursley

Epsom

Epsom, Surrey, monumental inscriptions: St. Martin's church, 1643-1960; Congregational Church, 1758-1874; Bugby Strict Baptist Chapel, 1787-1884. 8 fiche. East Surrey F.H.S. record publication **33**. 1990.

Ewhurst

JOHNSON, BRIAN, & JOHNSON, GILLIAN. 'Memorial inscriptions, Ewhurst', *R. & B.* **11**(2), 1984, 64-70; **11**(3), 1984, 103-6.

Farleigh

Farleigh. St. Mary the Virgin, Surrey. Monumental inscriptions 1495-1988. 1 fiche. East Surrey F.H.S. record publication **29**. 1990.

Farnham
See Thursley

Frimley
See Ash

Gatton

BROWN, A.O., et al. 'Memorial inscriptions: Gatton', *R. & B.* **6**(4), 1980, 144-7; **7**(1), 1980, 24-8.

Godalming

NEVILL, RALPH. 'Notes on the restoration of Godalming church', *Sy.A.C.* **7**, 1880, 277-87. Includes notes on monuments in the church.

Godalming, Hambledon, Chiddingfold, Dunfold. 2 fiche in folder. Monumental inscriptions on microfiche, **1**. West Surrey F.H.S., 1990.

Guildford

Guildford and Stoke. 1 fiche in folder. Monumental inscriptions on microfiche 2. West Surrey F.H.S., 1990.

The Old Mount Cemetery, Guildford: index of names on memorial inscriptions. [ ]: Guildford Archaeology Group/Surrey Archaeological Society, 1997.

Hambledon

See Godalming

Hascombe

See Shalford

Hersham

Monumental inscriptions: Saint Peter, Hersham (excluding the new churchyard). Paper 26. Walton & Weybridge Local History Society, 1988.

Horley

WALLER, J.G. 'On the monuments in Horley church', *Sy.A.C.* 7, 1880, 184-91. 14-15th c.

Horsell

WEBB, CLIFF, & WEBB, DIANE. 'Memorial inscriptions: Horsell', *R. & B.* 7(3 & 4), 1981, 102-11.

Horsell Common

WILCOCK, TIM. 'Horsell Common Chapel', *R. & B.* 19(3), 1992, 122. List of monumental inscriptions in a Baptist chapel.
See also Ash

Horsleys

See Byfleet

Ifield

ELLMAN, ERNEST. 'Ifield monumental inscriptions', *Sx.A.C.* 22, 1870, 214-20. See also 63, 1922, 237-8.

Kew

Kew, Surrey. Church of St. Anne monumental inscriptions 1714-1987. 2 fiche. East Surrey F.H.S. record publication 21. [1988?]

Kingston on Thames

BOCKETT, CHRISTINE. 'Monumental inscriptions in Kingston Baptist Church, Union Street', *E.Sy.F.H.S.J.* 18(2), 1995, 15-17.

All Saints church, Kingston upon Thames: memorials. [ ], [1995?]

Kingswood

Kingswood, St. Andrew, Surrey: monumental inscriptions, 1814-1987. 3 fiche. East Surrey F.H.S. record publication 28. 1990.

Lambeth

PARRY, G.S. 'Inscriptions in the churchyard of St. Mary's, Lambeth', *Notes & queries* 11th series 12, 1915, 296-7, 355-7, 396-8, 436-8 & 477-8. See also 449.

Leatherhead

BLAIR, W.J. 'A survey of churchyard monuments in the Leatherhead area', *P.L.D.L.H.S.* 3(6), 1972, 169-78; 3(7), 1973, 205-11; 3(8), 1974, 248-52; 3(9), 1975, 313-5; 4(1), 1977, 19-24.

SMITH, G.H. 'A history of the church and advowson of St. Mary and St. Nicholas, Leatherhead, chapter VII: monuments', *P.L.D.L.H.S.* 3(1), 1967, 33-5.

Merrow

See Byfleet

Merton

LEDGER, WALTER E. 'The hatchments in Merton church', *Wimbledon and Merton annual* 3, 1905, 53-66.

'Monumental inscriptions of the Merton Congregational Church, Morden Road', *E.Sy.F.H.S.J.* 19(4), 1996, 45.

Monumental inscriptions of the parish church of St. Mary the Virgin, Merton Park 1675-1995. 4 fiche in folder. East Surrey F.H.S. record publication M66. [199-.]

Mickleham

See Abinger

Mitcham

The church of St. Peter & St. Paul, Mitcham, Surrey, Diocese of Southwark: recordings of monumental inscriptions, 1583-1993. 7 fiche in folder. East Surrey F.H.S. record publication 47. [1993?]

Newington

HOVENDEN, ROBERT. *Monumental inscriptions in the old churchyard of St. Mary, Newington, Surrey.* 2 vols. Privately printed, 1880-1995. Pt. 2 published by the Society of Genealogists.

Nunhead

WOOLLACOTT, RON. *Nunhead notables: some of the interesting and important men and women buried in London's Nunhead Cemetery.* Nunhead: Friends of Nunhead Cemetery, 1984.

Oakwood

See Abinger

Ockham

DOWNING, N. ROSALINDE. 'Memorial inscriptions: Ockham', *R. & B.* 11(4), 1985, 143-6.

Ockham and Ockley. 2 fiche in folder. Monumental inscriptions on microfiche 5. West Surrey F.H.S., 1990.

Ockley

See Abinger and Ockham

Old Malden

Old Malden, Surrey. Church of St. John the Baptist. Monumental inscriptions, 1613-1979. East Surrey F.H.S. record publication 14. 1987.

Old Woking

WEBB, DIANE, & WEBB, CLIFF. 'Memorial inscriptions, Old Woking', *R. & B.* 7(2), 1980, 60-70.

See also Byfleet

Peper Harrow

HEALES, ALFRED. 'The brasses in Peper Harow church', *Sy.A.C.* 7, 1880, 34-43.

WEBB, CLIFFORD, & WEBB, DIANNE. 'Monumental inscriptions from the churchyard at Peper Harrow, Surrey', *R. & B.* 2(4), 1976, 156-7; 3(1), 1976, 16-17.

See also Compton

Petersham

ALDRED, MARGARET G. 'The monuments of a village church: Petersham, Surrey', *Monumental journal* 22(2), 1955, 108-10.

CRISP, F.A. 'Petersham, Surrey', *Fragmenta genealogica* 6, 1901, 45-148. Monumental inscriptions.

Pirbright

See Ash

Putney

CROTCH, ARTHUR. *Putney parish church of St. Mary the Virgin, Putney Bridge: its monuments and its story.* Wandsworth Borough News, 1936. Primarily inscriptions. For a reprint, see under Wimbledon below.

Monumental inscriptions of the old burial ground, Putney 1750-1854. 1 fiche in folder. East Surrey F.H.S. record publication **M68.** [199-?]

See also Wimbledon

Pyrford

See Wisley

Reigate

PICKANCE, J.W. 'Reigate church and monuments', *Sy.A.C.* 11, 1893, 185-203. In the church.

'Reigate church, Surrey', *Topographer* 3, 1790, 267-79. Includes monumental inscriptions, with list of 18th c. patrons and incumbents.

See also Abinger

Sanderstead

OUSELEY, M.H. 'Heraldry in All Saints church, Sanderstead', *L.H.R.* 8, 1969, 8-14; 9, 1970, 25-9.

Shalford

MESLEY, R.J. *South of Guildford.* 2 fiche in folder. Monumental inscriptions on microfiche 7. West Surrey F.H.S., 1993. Covers Shalford, Wonersh, Hascombe and Bramley.

Shirley

Monumental inscriptions of the parish church, St. John the Evangelist, Shirley, Surrey, 1803-1996. 5 fiche. East Surrey F.H.S. record publication **M69.** [199-].

See also Croydon

South Croydon
St. Peter, South Croydon, Surrey: memorial inscriptions, 1853-1987. 5 fiche in folder. East Surrey F.H.S. record publication **M71**. [199-.]

Southwark
BAX, ALFRED RIDLEY. 'On some armorial ledgers in the Cathedral Church of St. Saviour, Southwark, and the persons they commemorate', *Sx.A.C.* **22**, 1909, 1-68. Includes many wills, folded pedigrees of Corner, 18th c., and Kent, 18th c., and other brief pedigrees.

Stoke D'Abernon
ANTROBUS, MARY. 'The funeral surcoat in Stoke D'Abernon church', *Sy.A.C.* **46**, 1938, 59-67.

BOUTELL, CHARLES. 'On monumental brasses, with special notice of those at Stoke D'Abernon', *Sy.A.C.* **1**, 1858, 213-35.

CLIFT, J.G.N. 'The Stoke D'Abernon brasses', *Journal of the British Archaeological Association* N.S. **15**, 1909, 77-111.
See also Abinger

Streatham
BROMHEAD, H.W. *The heritage of St. Leonard's parish church, Streatham, being an account of the traditions and associations of the church.* Hatchards, 1932. Includes much information on monumental inscriptions.

Surbiton
CRESSWELL, FRANK, & CRESSWELL, JEAN. *Surbiton, Surrey: church of St. Mark monumental inscriptions.* 1 fiche in folder. East Surrey F.H.S. record publication **40**. 1989.

Tandridge
Tandridge, Surrey: parish church of St. Peter monumental inscriptions 1731-1988. 1 fiche in folder. East Surrey F.H.S. record publication **37**. [199-.]

Tatsfield
Tatsfield, Surrey: St. Mary's church monumental inscriptions 1711-1994. 2 fiche in folder. East Surrey F.H.S. record publication **55**. 1994.

Thames Ditton
EGAN, B.S.H. 'Brasses at Thames Ditton, Surrey, including a palimpsest find', *Transactions of the Monumental Brass Society* **10**(5), 1969, 378-83.

Thorpe
WEBB, CLIFF, & WEBB, DIANE. 'Monumental inscriptions in the church and churchyard of Thorpe, Surrey', *R. & B.* **5**(1), 1978, 31-3; **5**(2), 1978, 59-62.
See also Ash

Thursley
Thursley, Elstead, Farnham (The Bourne). 1 fiche in folder. Monumental inscriptions on microfiche **8**. West Surrey F.H.S., 1993.

Tilford
See Compton

Titsey
Titsey, St. James, Surrey. Monumental inscriptions, 1579-1988. 1 fiche. East Surrey F.H.S. record publications **31**. 1990.

Tooting Graveney
Monumental inscriptions of St. Nicholas church, Tooting Graveney, London, 1670-1989. 2 fiche in folder. East Surrey F.H.S. record publication **M67**. [199-.]

Walton on Thames
FORGE, J.W.LINDUS, & PULFORD, J.S.L. *Monumental inscriptions: Saint Mary, Walton-on-Thames.* Walton and Weybridge Local History Society paper **13**. 1974.

FORGE, J.W.LINDUS, & PULFORD, J.S.L. *Walton-on-Thames Cemetery: monumental inscriptions.* Walton & Weybridge Local History Society paper **24**. 1987.

Walton on the Hill
Walton on the Hill, Surrey: St. Peter the Apostle. Monumental inscriptions 1771-1971. 2 fiche in folder. East Surrey record publication **45**. [199-.]

Wanborough
See Compton and Wisley

Wandsworth

DAVIS, CECIL T. 'Monumental inscriptions in Wandsworth parish church', *M.G.H.* 3rd series, **5**, 1904, 273-9 & 290-95. With many notes.

West Horsley

WEBB, CLIFF. 'Memorial inscriptions from the churchyard at West Horsley, Surrey', *R. & B.* **4**(1), 1977, 11-13.

West Norwood

SMITH, ERIC E.F. 'The South Metropolitan Cemetery, West Norwood, and its memorials', in BIRD, JOANNA, CHAPMAN, HUGH, & CLARK, JOHN, eds. *Collectanea Londiniensia: studies in London archaeology and history presented to Ralph Merrifield.* Special paper, **2**. London and Middlesex Archaeological Society, 1978, 436-52. Includes list of memorials to persons listed in the *Dictionary of National Biography.*

SMITH, ERIC E.F. 'The South Metropolitan Cemetery, West Norwood, and its memorials', *Transactions of the London and Middlesex Archaeological Society* **30**, 1979, 152-86. Includes list of memorials to persons included in the *Dictionary of National Biography.*

FLANAGAN, BOB. *West Norwood Cemetery's sportsmen.* Friends of West Norwood Cemetery, 1995. Brief biographies of persons commemorated.

GRAHAM, PAUL. *West Norwood Cemetery: the Dickens connection.* Friends of West Norwood Cemetery, 1995. Notes on persons commemorated who were connected with Charles Dickens.

Westcott

See Abinger

Weybridge

FORGE, J.W.LINDUS. *Monumental inscriptions: Saint James, Weybridge.* Walton and Weybridge Local History Society paper **19**. 1979.

Whyteleafe

WILLIS, CHRISTOPHER. 'The memorials in St. Luke's Church, Whyteleafe', *L.H.R.* **33**, 1994, 9-13. Brief.

Monumental inscriptions of the parish church of St. Luke's, Whyteleafe, Surrey. 2 fiche in folder. East Surrey F.H.S. record publication **M72**. 1999.

'Are your ancestors buried at St. Luke's, Whyteleafe', *E.Sy.F.H.S.J.* **20**(2), 1997, 46. List of graves.

Wimbledon

ALDRED, MARGARET G. 'The memorials in St. Mary's church, Wimbledon', *Monumental journal.* **22**(5), 1955, 317-20.

ARNOLD, T.K. 'Heraldic and other glass in St. Mary's church, Wimbledon', *Wimbledon and Merton annual* **4**, 1910, 156-72.

CLARKE, A.W.HUGHES. *Monumental inscriptions in the church and churchyard of St. Mary's, Wimbledon.* Mitchell, Hughes and Clarke, 1934. Supplement to *M.G.H.*

Wimbledon and Putney, Surrey 1 fiche in folder. Monumental inscriptions on microfiche **9**. West Surrey F.H.S., 1996. Reprints the transcripts for Wimbledon by A.W.Hughes Clarke (1934), and for Putney by Arthur Crotch.

Windlesham

See Ash

Wisley

WEBB, CLIFF. 'Memorial inscriptions: Wisley, Bisley, Pyrford and Wanborough, Surrey', *R. & B.* **3**(3), 1977, 109-11.

Woking

ARNOLD, PHILLIP. *The memorials of St. Peter's, Woking, parish church, including some now lost.* Woking: Merlin Print, 1999. Brief pamphlet.

Woldingham

Woldingham, Surrey: St. Agatha's church monumental inscriptions, 1857-1979. 1 fiche. East Surrey F.H.S. monumental inscriptions, **16**. 1987.

Wonersh

See Shalford

Woodmansterne

Woodmansterne, Surrey: Parish church of St. Peter. Monumental inscriptions, 1771-1991. 1 fiche in folder. East Surrey F.H.S. record publication **43**. [199-].

Worplesdon

WEBB, DIANE, & WEBB, CLIFF. 'Memorial inscriptions: Worplesdon', *R. & B.* **9**(1), 1982, 25-32.
See also Compton

Wotton

See Abinger

SUSSEX
Albourne

HARRIS, JOAN. *Monumental inscriptions: Albourne & Woodmancote.* 1 fiche in folder. Microfiche series. [ ]: Sussex Family History Group 1992.

Aldingbourne

CLAYTON, CHARLES, E. 'Aldingbourne church', *Sx.A.C.* **37**, 1890, 191-3. Includes some monumental inscriptions.

Alfriston

NEWMAN, RONALD F. 'Monuments of Devonshire interest in a Sussex church: Alfriston', *Devon and Cornwall notes and queries* **32**(7), 1973, 216.

Battle

FAIRBANK, F.R. 'The brasses in Battle church Sussex', *Oxford journal of monumental brasses* **1**(3), 1897, 99-103.

Berwick

ELLMAN, EDWARD BOYS. 'Berwick', *Sx.A.C.* **12**, 1860, 254-5. Monumental inscriptions.

Bishopston

SIMMONS, HENRY. 'Monumental inscriptions, Bishopston, 1867', *Sx.A.C.* **19**, 1867, 185-8.

Bodiam

'Sepulchral brasses at Bodyam, Sussex', *Gentlemans magazine* N.S. **6**, 1837, 263-4.

Brighton

BISHOP, J.G. *Strolls in the Brighton Extra-Mural Cemetery, first and second series, 1864-67.* Brighton: Fleet & Co., 1867.

BURCHALL, MICHAEL J. 'Brighton's records lost and found', *Sx.F.H.* **1**(1), 1973, 7-8. Discussion of inscription transcription at St. Nicholas, Brighton.

JONES, MARTIN, D.W. 'Gothic enriched: Thomas Jackson's mural tablets in Brighton College Chapel', *Church monuments* **6**, 1991, 54-66. Jackson was the designer.

Broadwater

EXCELL, PHYL, & EXCELL, STANLEY. 'Monumental inscriptions at Broadwater', *Sx. F.H.* **4**(4), 1980, 119-21. Discussion of two 19th c. transcripts, by Hubert E. Snewin, and Edward Sayers.
See also West Tarring

Burgess Hill

POWELL, ROSE. 'St. John's Congregational Chapel, Burgess Hill: memorial inscriptions', *Sx.G.L.H.* **7**(1), 1985, 59-61.

PECKHAM, W.D. 'The General Baptist Chapel, Chichester', *Sx.N.Q.* **11**, 1946-7, 87-9. Monumental inscriptions.

Chichester

ALDSWORTH, FRED, & MCCANN, TIMOTHY J. 'Memorial inscriptions in the vault of the General Baptist chapel, Chichester', *W.Sx.H.* **19**, 1981, 4-7.

BLOXAM, M.H. 'Sepulchral effigies at Chichester', *Journal of the British Archaeological Asssociation* **42**, 1886, 287-93.

CODRINTON, PREBENDARY. 'Ancient coats of arms in Chichester Cathedral', *Sx.A.C.* **48**, 1905, 138-44.

EVERSHED, PETER. 'Some Eastgate, Chichester, Baptists', *Sx.F.H.* **13**(7), 1999, 254-6. Monumental inscriptions.

OSBORNE, NOEL H. *The epitaph book of William Hayley (1745-1820).* Chichester papers **49**. Chichester: Chichester City Council, 1965. The epitaphs relate to Chichester people.

SLAY, KATHERINE. *War memorials from Chichester, including stained glass, wall paques, and a roll of honour.* [ ]: Sussex Family History Group, 1995. Lists persons commemorated.

STEER, FRANCIS W. *The heraldic ceiling at the Bishop's Palace, Chichester.* Chichester papers **10**. Chichester: Chichester City Council, 1958.

Chiddingly

NOAKES, JAMES. 'Inscriptions in the church-yard, Chiddingly', *Sx.A.C.* **14**, 1862, 253-8.

Chithurst

See Rake

Cowdray

See Midhurst

Crawley

ELLMAN, ERNEST. 'Crawley monumental inscriptions', *Sx.A.C.* **24**, 1872, 301-3.

G., W.H. 'Sussex church plans XVII. Holy Trinity, Cuckfield', *Sx.N.Q.* **4**, 1933, 15-17. Plan of monuments in church, with a list.

Dicker

BURCHALL, MICHAEL J. Dicker Independent Chapel and M.I's.', *Sx.G.L.H.* **2**(2), 1980, 81-2.

Ditchling

ATTREE, F.W.T. 'Monumental inscriptions in Ditchling church and churchyard', *Sx.A.C.* **28**, 1878, 132-47.

Eartham

'Description of Eartham in Sussex, the seat of Wm. Haley, esq.', *Topographer* **4**, 1791, 228-32. Includes a few monumental inscriptions.

East Blatchington

DENNIS, R.N. 'Monumental insriptions, East Blatchington', *Sx.A.C.* **13**, 1861, 302.

East Grinstead

'Hatchments: an aspect of heraldry', *Bulletin of the East Grinstead Society* **39**, 1985, 4-6. Notes on hatchments at East Grinstead.

East Guldeford

SWARBROOKE, CHRIS. *St.Mary's church, East Guldeford: monumental inscriptions.* Record series **2**. Hastings: Hastings & Rother F.H.S., [1989].

East Hoathly

SEABROOK, JANE. *In loving memory: gravestone inscriptions and memorials in East Hoathly churchyard.* East Hoathly: C.T.R. Publishing, 1999.

Eastbourne

MEDHURST, L. & PITCHER, E. *Rolls of honour and war memorials in Eastbourne.* Eastbourne: Family Roots F.H.S. (Eastbourne & District), 1994.

Index to 1914-1918 war memorial of Eastbourne, East Sussex. Eastbourne: P.B.N. Publications, 1989.

St. Mary's parish church, Eastbourne, Sussex: monumental inscriptions. 1 fiche in folder. [ ]: Sussex Family History Group, 1998.

St. Mary's parish church, Eastbourne, Sussex: monumental inscriptions. Eastbourne: P.B.N. Publications, 1998.

Falmer

See Stanmer

Ferring

'History of Ferring, in Sussex', *Topographer* **3**, 1790, 156-63 & 209-14. Includes monumental inscriptions.

Goring

SIDNEY, J. 'Some account of Goring church', *Gentleman's magazine* **78**, 1808, 121. Includes brief note on inscriptions.

Hailsham

GRIMALDI, A.B. 'Hailsham monumental inscriptions', *Sx.G.L.H.* **1**(1), 1979, 24-7. Recorded in 1869.

Hangleton

SNELL, F.S. 'Monumental inscriptions of Hangleton church (St. Helen's) and churchyard, Sussex', *M.G.H.* 2nd series **1**, 1886, 341-2.

Hastings

BAX, ALFRED RIDLEY. 'Inscriptions in the churchyard of All Saints, Hastings', *Sx.A.C.* **40**, 1896, 236-51; **41**, 1898, 216-31; **43**, 1900, 252-75.

BAX, ALFRED RIDLEY. *Croft Chapel, Hastings: monumental inscriptions in the burial ground, plus tablets in the chapel.* Record series **15**. Hastings: Hastings & Rother F.H.S., 1998.

BAX ALFRED RIDLEY. *St.Clement's church, Hastings: monumental inscriptions in the churchyard plus burials in the crypt.* Record series **14**. Hastings: Hastings & Rother F.H.S., 1998.

BAX, ALFRED RIDLEY. 'Inscriptions in the churchyard and crypt of St. Clements, and in the Croft Chapel and burial ground, Hastings', *Sx.A.C.* **49**, 1906, 105-25. This is reprinted in the two works just cited.

CHALLEN, FREDERICK K. *St.Mary-in-the-Castle: burials in the crypt and monumental inscriptions,* ed. C. Swarbrooke. Record series **11a**. Hastings: Hastings & Rother F.H.S., 1995.

MEDHURST, L., & PITCHER, E. *War memorials in Hastings.* Eastbourne: Family Roots F.H.S. (Eastbourne & District), 1992.

'St. Mary's, Hastings, M.I's', *Sx.G.L.H.* **2**(1), 1980, 40-44.

Hastings Cemetery records. Register no.1. 02 December 1856-10 Dec. 1866. 1 fiche in folder. Hastings: Hastings & Rother F.H.S., 1998.

Hastings Cemetery records. Register no.2. 12 Dec.1866-12 Sep.1872. 1 fiche in folder. Hastings: Hastings & Rother F.H.S., 1998.

St. Clement's church (Halton), Hastings, 1838-1970: monumental inscriptions. Hastings: Hastings & Rother F.H.S., 1987.

Hellingly. Horselunges

LOWER, MARK ANTONY. 'Accout of moated manor house of Horselunges', *Gentleman's magazine* N.S. **23**, 1845, 271-2. Notes on heraldic glass in a farmhouse at Hellingly.

Henfield

Monumental inscriptions: Henfield & Shermanbury. 1 fiche in folder. Microfiche series. [ ]: Sussex Family History Group, 1992.

Herstmonceux

KINNISON, JUDITH. 'Herstmonceaux Congregational Chapel: a record of the memorial inscriptions & graves', *Sx.G.L.H.* **3**(4), 1981, 120-124.

Hooe

GOWER, LEN. *St.Oswalds church, Hooe: monumental inscriptions.* Publication **5**. Hastings: Hastings & Rother F.H.S., 1992.

Horsham

SLYFIELD, G.N. 'Scheduling of head and footstones in the closed churchyard of St Mary's, Horsham', *Sx.N.Q.* **13**, 1950-53, 215.

Horsted Keynes

LEVESON GOWER, GRANVILLE. 'Monumental inscriptions from the church of Horsted Keynes, Sussex', *Sx.A.C.* **34**, 1886, 107-20.

LEVESON GOWER, GRANVILLE. 'Monumental inscriptions from the church of Horstead Keynes, Sussex', *M.G.H.* 2nd series **1**, 1886, 159-64.

Icklesham

WICKING, BENITA. *All Saints church, Icklesham: monumental inscriptions in the churchyard plus tablets in the church.* Hastings: Hastings & Rother F.H.S., 1998.

BUTLER, G. SLADE. 'Inscriptions in Icklesham church, 1862', *Sx.A.C.* **14**, 1862, 259-62. And in the churchyard.

Iping
See Rake

Isfield

'Account of Isfield, Sussex', *Topographer* **4**, 1791, 336-42. Mainly monumental inscriptions.

Jevington

Monumental inscriptions of St. Andrew's church, Jevington, Sussex. [Eastbourne]: Family Roots F.H.S. (Eastbourne & District), [1991].

Kirdford

DUNKIN, E.H.W. 'Kirdford M.I's', *Sx.F.H.* **3**(5), 1978, 146-7. Recorded in 1892.

Lewes

MEDHURST, L., & PITCHER, E. *Rolls of honour and war memorials in Lewes, Peacehaven, and Piddinghoe.* [Eastbourne]: Family Roots F.H.S. (Eastbourne & District), 1993.

Lewes men whose names are entered in bronze on the Lewes War Memorial at School Hill, Lewes, 1914-1918. Eastbourne: Family Roots F.H.S. (Eastbourne & District), 1991.

Lindfield

BAX, ALFRED RIDLEY. 'Inscriptions in the church and church-yard of Lindfield, Co.Sussex', *Sx.A.C.* **37**, 1890, 151-72.

Littlehampton
NEWMAN, RONALD F. *Monumental inscriptions in the parish church of St. Mary the Virgin, Littlehampton.* Littlehampton papers 3. Littlehampton: Littlehampton Urban District Council, 1970.

Littleworth
'War memorial on the B2135 opposite Mill Lane, Littleworth, West Sussex', *Sx.F.H.* 8(8), 1989, 340. Memorial to World War I casualties of the West Grinstead area.

Lynch
See Rake

Midhurst
Q., Q. 'Epitaphs in the church of Midhurst, Sussex', *Gentlemans magazine* 73(2), 1803, 922. See also 1121.

Midhurst
'An account of Midhurst and Cowdry, in Sussex', *Topographer* 4, 1791, 270-80. Mainly monumental inscriptions.

Mid Lavant
GOWER, ARTHUR F.G. 'Inscriptions in Mid Lavant church', *M.G.H.* 4th series 3, 1910, 203.

Milland
See Rake

New Shoreham
SALMON, ERNEST FREDK. 'Inscriptions in New Shoreham church', *Sx.A.C.* 52, 1909, 156-62.

Newtimber
'Newtimber M.I's, 1896', *Sx.G.L.H.* 1(2), 1979, 64.

North Mundham
'History of North Mundham, Sussex', *Topographer* 4, 1791, 220-28. Mainly monumental inscriptions; also includes a few parish register extracts.

Norway
MILLER, VI. 'Memorial inscriptions found in St. Andrews church, Norway, Eastbourne', *F.R.* 3(2), 1988, 11-12. Predominantly names from the roll of honour, 1914-1918 world war.

Peacehaven
See Lewes

Pett
WICKING, BENITA. *St.Mary and St.Peter's church, Pett: monumental inscriptions.* Publication 23. Hastings: Hastings & Rother F.H.S., 2000.

Petworth
Q., Q. 'Petworth', *Gentlemans magazine* 73(2), 1803, 922.

Piddinghoe
See Lewes

Plumpton
'Plumpton M.I's, *Sx.F.H.* 3(6), 1978, 186-9.

Poynings
HAMMOND, N.D. 'The lost brasses of Poynings, Sussex', *Transactions of the Monumental Brass Society* 10(2), 1964, 85-9.

HOLLAND, STEWART. 'Inscriptions in the parish curch and churchyard of Poynings', *Sx.A.C.* 15, 1863, 231-3.

Preston
Monumental inscriptions: Preston & West Blatchington. 1 fiche in folder. Microfiche series, **PF23.** [ ]: Sussex Family History Group, 1993.

Pulborough
'An account of Pulborough, in Sussex', *Topographer* 4 1791, 333-9.

Racton
ARNOLD, F.H. 'Racton monumental inscriptions', *Sx.A.C.* 23, 1871, 314-7.

Rake
Memorials of wars: in two world wars, these men from Rake, Milland, Lynch, Iping and Chithurst died, securing and defending freedom for others. Tuxlith tracts 2. Milland: Friend of Tuxlith Chapel, 1995.

Ringmer
BRIDGER, GEOFFREY. *Valiant hearts of Ringmer: Ringmer war memorial.* Ringmer: the author, 1993. Biographies of war casualties.

'An account of Ringmer in Sussex',
Topographer 4 1791, 281-300. Mainly
monumental inscriptions.

Rusper
ELLMAN, ERNEST. 'Rusper monumental
insriptions', *Sx.A.C.* **25**, 1873, 220-24.
*The men who marched away: a remembrance
of the men whose names are recorded on
the Rusper war memorial.* Rusper: Avery's
Press, 1981.

Rustington
LEESON, F.L. 'Buried gravestone in
Rustington church', *Sx.F.H.* **13**(1), 1998, 23.

Rye
BUTLER, G. SLADE. 'The vicars of Rye and
their patrons: with the mural, slab, and
headstone inscriptions in the parish
church and church-yard of St. Mary, and
the Baptist chapel, Rye', *Sx.A.C.* **13**, 1861,
270-301.
EWART, PETER, & EWART, LYNNE.
*Monuments to memory: the story of Rye's
war memorials.* Hawkhurst: Ewart
Publications, 1988. Includes list of persons
commemorated.
RYE LOCAL HISTORY GROUP. *Rye Cemetery
index of marked graves, Including
illustrations of interesting gravestones.*
Rye: Rye Local History Group, 1996.

Salehurst
FIELD, C.W. 'Salehurst, East Sussex, M.I's',
Sx.F.H. **4**(3), 1980, 100-106.

Seaford
SIMMONS, HENRY. 'Monumental inscriptions,
Seaford', *Sx.A.C.* **12**, 1860, 242-53.

Shermanbury
See Henfield

Slaugham
WARDEN, STEPHEN. 'Slaugham M.I's',
Sx.G.L.H. **1**(3), 1979, 110-11.

Stanmer
Stanmer & Falmer monumental inscriptions.
2 fiche in folder. Microfiche series. [ ]:
Sussex Family History Group, 1992.

Stopham
'History of Stopham, Sussex', *Topographer* **4**,
1791, 346-53. Monumental inscriptions.
HAMPER, WILLIAM. 'Street church',
Gentlemans magazine **74**, 1804, 1181-2.
Mainly inscriptions.

Treyford
TROKE, R. CHARLES. 'Old Treyford church',
Sx.N.Q. **10**, 1944-5, 178-81. Mainly
inscriptions.

Upper Dicker
*Monumental inscriptions of Zoar Baptist
Chapel, Upper Dicker, nr. Hailsham, East
Sussex* Eastbourne: Family Roots F.H.S.,
1986.

Wadhurst. Shovers Green
KINNISON, JUDITH, & HARWOOD, BRIAN.
'Shovers Green Chapel, Wadhurst: the past,
the pastors, and memorial inscriptions',
Sx.G.L.H. **3**(2), 1981, 56-60.

Wartling
*Monumental inscriptions, St. Mary
Magdalene church, Wartling, Sussex.*
Eastbourne: Family Roots F.H.S.
(Eastbourne & District), 1992.

West Blatchington
See Preston

West Dean
'An account of Westdean in Sussex',
Topographer 4 1791, 265-70. Notes on
heraldry, *etc.*

West Grinstead
'The church and monuments at West
Grinstead', *Sx.G.L.H.* **5**(1), 1983, 18-21.

West Tarring
SAYERS, EDWARD. *Transcripts of, and
extracts from, records of the past.*
Worthing: W.J.C. Long, 1903. Monumental
inscriptions of West Tarring, Broadwater,
and Christ Church, Worthing.

Westbourne
SPERLING, JOHN HANSON. 'Westbourne
monumental inscriptions in the church,
churchyard and cemetery', *Sx.A.C.* **22**,
1870, 201-13. See also **23**, 1871, 324.

Willingdon
BAX, ALFRED RIDLEY. 'Inscriptions in the churchyard of Willingdon, Co.Sussex', *Sx.A.C.* **34**, 1886, 221-36.

St. Mary's church, Willingdon, Sussex: monumental inscriptions in church and churchyard. Eastbourne: Family Roots F.H.S. (Eastbourne & District), 1994.

Woodmancote
See Albourne

Worth
GORE, R.C.W. *The parish church of Saint Nicholas, Worth, West Sussex: the 1914-1918 war memorial. A remembrance of the men of the parish of Worth who died during the Great War.* Crawley: R.C.W. Gore, 1996.

Worthing
See West Tarring

C. Individual and Family Inscriptions

Abbott
KING, THOS. WM. 'Remarks on a brass plate formerly in the church of the Holy Trinity at Guildford, and now remaining in the Hospital there', *Sy.A.C.* **3**, 1865, 254-9. Abbott family memorial, 1606; includes extracts from Guildford parish registers, 1558-1654, funeral certificates and wills of Abbott family, and pedigree, 17th c.

PALMER, PHILIP G. *The Knight of the Red Cross, or, the romance of Archbishop Abbot's tomb in the church of the Holy and Undivided Trinity, Guildford, Surrey.* Guildford: Frank Lasham, 1911.

Atkins
GROVER, J.W. 'Discovery of the Atkins monument at Clapham', *Journal of the British Archaeological Association* **42**, 1886, 272-8. 17th c.

Bartelot
STEER, FRANCIS W. 'Heraldic glass in Stopham church, Sussex, England', *New England historical and genealogical register* **112**, 1958, 308-12. Memorials of the Bartelot family.

Benge
HODGKINSON, J.S. 'Further additions to the catalogue of early Wealden iron graveslabs', *Wealden iron: bulletin of the Wealden Iron Research Group* 2nd series, **14**, 1994, 28-9. Graveslab of Lucy Benge, 1689, of Laughton, Sussex.

Boughen
GODFREY, WALTER H. 'The burial place of Edward Boughen', *Sx.N.Q.* **6**, 1936-7, 52. 1660; in Southease church.

Bowthe
EGAN, B.S.H. 'The repaired brass of Bishop Bowthe at East Horsley, Surrey', *Transactions of the Monumental Brass Society* **11**, 1969-74, 147-8. 1478.

Bridger
SPONG, JUNE. 'One hundred and eleven years', *Sx.F.H.* **11**(8), 1995, 285. Bridger family tombstones at Mitcham, Surrey.

Buc
STEER, FRANCIS W. 'A parchment memorial in Chichester Cathedral', *Sx.N.Q.* **16**, 1963-7, 1-4. Memorial to Robert Buc of Long Melford, 1579.

Burré
LOWER, MARK ANTONY. 'The tomb of Richard Burré in Sompting church', *Sx.A.C.* **19**, 1867, 180-84. 1527-8.

Burton
NEWMAN, RONALD F. 'The Burton monument in Kingston Cemetery', *Sy.A.C.* **68**, 1971, 204-5. Early 20th c.

Camoys
EXCELL, STANLEY. 'The Camoys brass at Trutton', *Sx.F.H.* **8**(4), 1988, 159-62. 15th c.

Carew
SMITH, J.C.CHALLENOR. 'A note on the brass to Philip Carew, 1414, at Beddington', *Sy.A.C.* **43**, 1935, 53-60. Includes will of Arthur Ormsby, 1468.

'Nicholas Carew and wife Isabel, 1432: Beddington, Surrey', *Portfolio of the Monumental Brass Society* **2**(12), 1905, plate 59. Illustration only.

Carleton

ESDAILE, MRS. 'An incised slab at Cuckfield', *Sx.A.C.* **82,** 1942, 96-103. Memorial of Carleton and Vicars families, 17th c.

Caryll

L[OWER], M.A. 'Monumental inscriptions to John Caryll, in the College des Ecossais, Paris', *Sx.A.C.* **19,** 1867, 191-2. Of Hastings; 1711.

Cheyham

MARSHALL, CHARLES J. 'Brass in Lumley Chapel, Cheam', *Sy.A.C.* **47,** 1941, 100-101. Commemorating William de Cheyham, 1347.

Chillingworth

PECKHAM, W.D. 'The epitaph of William Chillingworth', *Sx.N.Q.* **12,** 1948-9, 79-83. 1643/4.

Clarke

GARDNER, ERIC. 'A recently discovered tablet from Weybridge old church', *Sy.A.C.* **28,** 1915, 186. Relating to the Clarke, Sutton, and Inwood families, late 16th c.

Clerk

See Prestwick

Coade

PLENNEY, ALAN. 'Coade and Sealy: within this vault', *E.Sy.F.H.S.J.* **15**(1), 1992, 18-20. Description of a family vault at St. Mary's, Lambeth.

Cobham

WALLER, J.G. 'Notes on the monuments of the Cobham family at Lingfield', *Sy.A.C.* **5,** 1871, 186-99.

Cole

GOLLIN, G.J. 'George Cole of Pryors Farm, or Little Ashtead manor', *P.L.D.L.H.S.* **4**(8), 1984, 225-6. Note on monument in Petersham church, 1624.

Cotton

'Robert Cotton, 1591, and wife, Grace, Richmond, Surrey', *Portfolio of the Monumental Brass Society* **2**(11), 1905, plate 55. Illustration only.

Covert

D'ELBOUX, R.H. 'The Covert brasses, Slaugham', *Sx.N.Q.* **14,** 1954-7, 80-82. 15-16th c.

Cox

WINBOLT, S.E. 'Brass to Dr. W. Cox in Tillington church', *Sx.N.Q.* **4,** 1933, 91-2. 1656.

Cranford

CLIFT, J.G.N. 'Brass of Edward Cranford', *Journal of the British Archaeological Association* N.S. **14,** 1908, 263-5. At Puttenham, 1431.

D'Abernon

EGAN, BRIAN. 'Repairing the brsass of Sir John D'Abernon the younger, 1327, at Stoke D'Abernon, Surrey', *Transactions of the Monumental Brass Society* **12**(1), 1975, 51-2.

Dacre

RAY, JOHN E. 'The parish church of All Saints, Herstmonceux, and the Dacre tomb', *Sx.A.C.* **58,** 1916, 21-64. See also 198-200. The tomb generally thought to be that of the Fenys or Fynes family. Includes folded pedigree of Fynes, Dacre and Lennard, 13-17th c., shewing relationships; also will of John Pencell, 1485.

Dallingridge

EGAN, B.S.H. & MORRIS, R.K. 'A restoration at Fletching, Sussex: the Dallingridge tomb', *Transactions of the Monumental Brass Society* **10**(6), 1970, 436-44.

Delve(s)

DUNKIN, E.H.W. 'On an incised memorial slab in Little Horsted churchyard', *Sx.A.C.* **26,** 1875, 216-8. Delve family, c.1500.

ESDAILE, MRS. 'Two Sussex monuments, 1: the Delves monument, Horsham', *Sx.N.Q.* **8,** 1940-41, 97-8. 1654.

Elrington

THOMAS-STANFORD, C. 'The tomb of Edward Elrington at Preston', *Brighton and Hove archaeologist* **2,** 1924, 73-80. 1515.

Evershed

EVERSHED, PETER. 'The grave of a living memorial', *W.Sx.H.* **55**, 1995, 32. Evershed family memorial at Billingshurst, 19th c.

Fenys

See Dacre

Fettiplace

DUNLOP, J. RENTON. 'Brasses commemorative of the Fettiplace family', *Transactions of the Monumental Brass Society* **6**(2), 1911, 95-119. In Berkshire, Buckinghamshire, Oxfordshire and Sussex.

Fitz Alan

FOSTER, PAUL, BRIGHTON, TREVOR, & GARLAND, PATRICK. *An Arundel tomb.* Otter memorial paper **1**. Chichester: Bishop Otter College Trustees, 1987. Probably of Richard Fitz Alan, Earl of Arundel, 1376.

Foster

TURNER, FREDERIC. 'The monument to Chief Justice Foster in Egham church', *Sy.A.C.* **19**, 1906, 199-200. 1663.

Francis

See Gittins

Fynes

See Dacre

Gage

ESDAILE, MRS. 'The Gage monument at Firle and their author', *Sx.N.Q.* **8**, 1940-41, 162-4. 16-17th c.

'The Gage monuments, Firle', *Sx.N.Q.* **2**, 1929, 175-7. See also 215-6. 16th c.

Gittins

FLEMING, LINDSAY. 'M.I. in Edgefield church, Norfolk', *Sx.N.Q.* **17**, 1968-71, 56-7. Inscriptions to Jane Gittins of South Stoke, 1779, and to Bransby Francis of Edgefield, 1829.

Goring

See Clerk

Gott

See Saunder(s)

Grey

WILLATTS, R.M. 'Dame Katherine and her rescued husbands', *Bulletin of the East Grinstead Society* **29**, 1980, 11-13. See also **42**, 1987, 5-8. Brass to memory of Katherine Grey nee Lewknor, 1505.

Hardyng

BINGLEY, A.H. 'Monument of Robert Hardyng in St. Nicholas Church, Cranleigh', *Sy.A.C.* **37**, 1926-7, 101. Brief note, 1503.

Hassard

GODFREY, WALTER H. 'Effigies and arms of Hassard, All Saints, Lewes', *Sx.N.Q.* **3**, 1929, 58-9. 1624.

Heron

STEPHENSON, MILL. 'Notes on the brass of William Heron, esq., and wife Alice, lately replaced in Croydon church', *Sy.A.C.* **10**, 1891, 134-9. 1562; includes list of other brasses at Croydon.

Howard

SMITH, J. CHALLENOR. 'Lady Howard's monument in Richmond church', *Sy.A.C.* **10**, 1891, 288-92. 1716; includes pedigree, 16-18th c.

Ifield

ELLIS, W.S. 'Effigies in Ifield church', *Sx.A.C.* **8**, 1856, 267-8. Ifield family, 14th c.

Inwood

See Clarke

Jefferay

LOOSEMORE, JOSE. 'The Jefferay monument in Chiddingly church', *Sx.F.H.* **11**(5), 1995, 163. 17th c.

SPERLING, JOHN H. 'Jefferay monument, Chiddingly', *Sx.A.C.* **18**, 1866, 193-4. List of arms.

Johnson

LEVESON GOWER, ARTHUR F.G. 'Monumental inscriptions at Singleton in Sussex', *M.G.H.* 4th series, **3**, 1910, 142. Memorial to Thomas Johnson, 1744.

Keynes

WALFORD, WESTON STYLEMAN. 'The small cross-legged effigy at Horsted Keynes, Sussex, with some notice of the ancient family of Keynes', *Sx.A.C.* **1**, 1848, 128-41. Includes pedigree of Keynes, 13th c.

Kington

'The Kington brass, 1597', *Sx.N.Q.* **6**, 1936-7, 149-50.

La Warre

BURGES, W. 'The tomb and helm of Thomas La Warre in the church at Broadwater, Sussex', *Archaeological journal* **36**, 1879, 78-87. 1526.

Legatt

SLATFORD, JOHN. 'Discovery of a forgotten tombstone in Send church', *Send & Ripley History Society newsletter* **65**, 1985, 5-6. To Jeremiah Legatt, 1708; includes notes on family.

Lethieuller

MARKHAM, SARAH. 'The Lethieullier tombe at Clapham', *Transactions of the London and Middlesex Archaeological Society* **35**, 1987, 135-48.

Leveson-Gower

'Monument to the late Granville Leveson-Gower in Titsey church', *Sy.A.C.* **16**, 1901, 253. Brief note.

Lewknor

See Grey

Long

FYNMORE, A.H.W. 'Long family of Jamaica', *Notes & queries* **165**, 1933, 339-40. Monumental inscriptions; of Jamaica, Surrey and Wiltshire.

Lumley

CLINCH, GEORGE. 'Notes on the Lumley monuments at Cheam', *Sy.A.C.* **22**, 1909, 162-7. 16-17th c.

DUNK, HERBERT. 'The Lumley monuments in the ancient church of St. Dunstan, Cheam, Surrey', *Transactions of the Ancient Monuments Society* N.S., **2**, 1954, 93-107. 16-17th c.

Lyfelde

PRICE, R.G. 'Lyfelde monument at Stoke D'Abernon', *Reliquary* **13**, 1872-3, 255-6. Monumental inscription, 1592, with pedigree.

Manning

See Whitfield

May

ALDSWORTH, F.G. 'The May family vault and the Lady May monument in the church of St. Nicholas, Mid Lavant, West Sussex', *Sx.A.C.* **120**, 1982, 231-4. Includes May family pedigree, 16-17th c.

BAYLEY, T.D.S. 'Lady Mary May's monument in Mid Lavant church', *Sx.A.C.* **107**, 1969, 1-11. Late 17th c.

ESDAILE, MRS. 'The May monument, Mid Lavant', *Sx.N.Q.* **8**, 1940-41, 129-32. 17th c.

Norbury

STEPHENSON, MILL. 'On a brass in Stoke D'Abernon church', *Sy.A.C.* **10**, 1891, 283-7. Commemorating Lady Anna, wife of Sir Henry Norbury, 1464. Includes pedigree, 15th c.

Ottaway

BUCKLAND, LESLIE, & BUCKLAND, MURIEL. 'Monumental find at Danehill', *Sx.G.L.H.* **2**(1), 1980, 21-6. Ottaway family, 17-18th c.

Owen

BLAAUW, W.H. 'On the effigy of Sir David Owen in Easeborne church, near Midhurst ... to which his will and codicil are now added', *Sx.A.C.* **7**, 1854, 22-43. Includes pedigree, 15-16th c. Will dated 1529.

Paine

HEWETT, MARY. 'Burial vault in Frensham church', *F.M.S.Q.N.* **8**(6), 1988, 123-5. Paine family vault, with notes on family, 17-19th c.

Pelham

SMITH, L.B. 'The Pelham vault', *Sussex county magazine* **4**, 1930, 370-72. Includes list of persons buried, 17-18th c.

Philcox

MAY, GWEN. 'Philcox family history on gravestones', *F.R.* **12**(1), 1997, 11-12. At Hartfield, 19th c.

Pitt

NEVILL, EDM. 'Pitt family from Ilminster, Somerset', *Notes & queries for Somerset & Dorset* **11**, 1909, 332. Memorial inscriptions at Wimbledon, 17-19th c.

Poole

LAMBARDE, FANE. 'The Poole memorial in Ditchling church', *Sx.N.Q.* **3**, 1931, 204-5. 1580.

Porter

EVANS, TONY. 'The Porter family, lords of Allfarthing manor', *Wandsworth historian* **68**, 1997, 8. Note on a memorial plaque to John Porter, 1767.

Powlett

TOWNSEND, JOHN. 'The Powlett monument, West Grinstead', *Sx.F.H.* **14**(3), 2000, 99. 18th c.

Prestwick

ANDRE, J. LEWIS. 'Notes on three Sussex brasses', *Sx.A.C.* **36**, 1888, 172-9. Brasses of Williams Prestwick, 1436, at Warbleton, Thomas Clerk(?) 1411, at Horsham, and Lady Elizabeth Goring, 1558, at Burton.

Roberts

NEWMAN, RONALD F. 'Monuments of Devonshire interest in a Sussex church: Littlehampton', *Devon and Cornwall notes and queries* **31**, 1968-70, 181. Monumental inscription to Jemima Roberts of Barnstaple, 1834.

Rowed

BROADBENT, UNA. 'The Rowed monument at Coulsdon', *L.H.R.* **10**, 1971, 21-4. Early 17th c.

Sackville

ESDAILE, MRS. 'Notes on the Sackville monumets in Withyham church', *Sx.N.Q.* **4**, 1933, 120-21. 17-18th c.

ESDAILE, !MRS. 'Some Sussex monuments III. Cibber's Sackville monument at Withyham', *Sx.N.Q.* **8**, 1940-41, 185-7. 17th c.

N., J.G. 'Sepulchral memorials of the Sackville family at Withyam, Sussex', *Collectanea topographica et genealogica* **3**, 1836, 295-306. 15-18th c.; includes parish register extracts.

Samuelson

GRANT, JOY. 'The strange story of the Samuelson mausoleum at Hatchford Park', *Surrey history* **5**(2), 1995, 76-83. 20th c.

Saunder(s)

EGAN, B.S.H., & HUTCHINSON, ROBERT. 'The Saunder brass at Charlwood, Surrey', *Transactions of the Monumental Brass Society* **11**, 1969-74, 402-6. 1553.
'Streat parish and Wealden iron', *Sx.G.L.H.* **7**(1), 1985, 29-30. Graveslabs of Sarah Saunders, 1761, and Martha Gott, 1732.

Sealy

See Coade

Sefton

ARNOLD, F.H. 'Monumental inscription in Bignor church', *Sx.A.C.* **39**, 1894, 207. Thomas Sefton, 1671.

Selden

GODFREY, WALTER H. 'John Selden's tomb in the Temple Church', *Sx.N.Q.* **13**, 1950-53, 97-8. 1654.

Selwyn

'The Selwyn monument, Friston', *Sx.N.Q.* **2**, 1929, 15-16. c.1613.

Skayles

HENRY, MICK. 'An impressive gravestone', *Sx.F.H.* **11**(1), 1994, 3. Daniel Skayles, 1796, at Patcham.

Skern

'Robert Skern, 1437, and wife, Kingston-upon-Thames, Surrey. *Portfolio of the Monumental Brass Society* **2**(2), 1900, plate 9. Illustration only.

Stanford

'The Thomas-Stanford Trust Fund', *Sx.A.C.* **74**, 1933, 226-41. Includes many monumental inscriptions of the Stanford family 18-20th c.; also will of Sir Charles Thomas-Stanford, 1932. Part of the trust's responsibility is to maintain the monuments.

Stansfield

GODFREY, WALTER H. 'The Stansfield effigies, Lewes', *Sx.N.Q.* **7**, 1938-9, 1-2. 17th c.

Sutton

See Clarke

Tettersell

'[Captn. Nicholas Tettersell's epitaph at Brighton]', *Gentlemans magazine* **43**, 1773, 17. See also 127. 1674

Warham

STEINMAN, GEORGE STEINMAN. 'The Warham monument in Croydon church', *Sy.A.C.* **1**, 1858, 57-60. Memorial to Hugh Warham, c.1537.

War(r)en(n)e

ANDERSON, F. 'William of warenne's tombstone', *Sx.A.S.N.* **50**, 1986, 515. 11th c.

D'ELBOUX, R.H. 'The Warren(?) shield at St. Michaels, Lewes', *Sx.N.Q.* **9**, 1942-3, 123-4. Medieval.

NORRIS, MALCOLM. 'St. Michael's, Lewes, Sussex: a connection', *Transactions of the Monumental Brass Society* **11**, 1969-74, 260-61. Warrenne family, early 15th c.

Whitfield

THRELFALL, JOHN B. 'A shield of arms at Worth', *Sx.F.H.* **5**, 1982, 65-7. Memorial to Thomas Whitfield and his wife Mildred, nee Manning, 1630.

Wybarne

GAUNT, CHARLES. 'On the brass of John Wybarne, A.D. 1490, lately discovered in Ticehurst church, with some account of his family and of the church', *Sx.A.C.* **8**, 1856, 17-30. 1490; includes pedigree, 15-16th c.

3. PROBATE RECORDS, INQUISITIONS POST MORTEM, etc.

A. *General*

Probate records - wills, inventories, administration bonds, accounts, *etc.,* are invaluable sources of genealogical information. A wide variety of indexes, calendars etc. for Surrey and Sussex are available. There are two major general listings for Surrey:

WEBB, CLIFF. ed. *Union index of Surrey probate records which survive from before the year 1650.* Index Library **99**. British Record Society, 1990. Alternative title: *Surrey probate records to 1649.*

HOLMAN, JOAN, & HERRIDGE, MARION. *Index of Surrey probate inventories, 16th-19th centuries.* Epsom: Domestic Buildings Research Group (Surrey), 1986. Indexes 6,000 documents from all courts with jurisdiction in Surrey.

See also:

'Surrey probate material', *E.Sy.F.H.S.J.* 4(2), 1981, 14-16. General discussion of their whereabouts, now rather dated.

WEBB, CLIFF. 'Early Surrey wills', *R. & B.* 24(1), 1997, 10-14. General discussion of pre 1649 Surrey wills.

ALLINSON, HELEN. 'Inventories', *R. & B.* 15(4), 1989, 136-7. Brief general discussion. *Elizabethan Surrey probate inventories.* Sy.R.S., forthcoming.

For Sussex, see:

BURCHALL, M.J. *A guide to Sussex probate records.* Occasional papers **7**. Brighton: Sussex Genealogical Centre, 1981. Guide to the various probate courts.

MCCANN, TIMOTHY J. *West Sussex probate inventories 1521-1834: a catalogue.* Booklet with 4 fiche. Chichester: West Sussex County Council, 1981.

CROOKSHANK, A.C. 'Wills of Sussex clergy', *Sx.N.Q.* **8**, 1940-41, 198-201; **9**, 1942-3, 15-16, 42-3, 67-9 & 96. List from Index Library **49** & **64** (See below, p.50.).

NIGHTINGALE, JOHN. 'Sussex wills beneficiaries index', *Sx.F.H.* **13**(2), 1998, 37-41; **13**(3), 1998, 83-5, **13**(4), 1998, 114-21. Index to beneficiaries in the wills from 7 West Sussex parishes i.e. Shirley, West Chiltington, Kirdford, Washington, Pulborough, West Grinstead.

RICE, R. GARRAWAY. *Transcripts of Sussex wills, as far as they relate to ecclesiological and parochial subjects, up to the year 1560, transcribed and classified*, ed. Walter H. Godfrey. 4 vols. Sx.R.S. **41-3** & **45**. 1935-46. Extracts rather than full transcripts.

SALZMAN, L.F. 'Sussex wills in the Record Office and British Museum', *Sx.N.Q.* **6**, 1936-7, 41-3. List of wills filed with 'ancient deeds' or amongst the British Library's additional manuscripts.

'[Brief list of non-official probate inventories at East Sussex Record Office]', *Sx.G.L.H.* **1**(3), 1979, 76.

'Stray inventories at W.S.R.O.', *Sx.G.L.H.* **2**(3), 1980, 117. Brief list.

Prerogative Court of Canterbury

The P.C.C. had over-riding probate jurisdiction throughout England, and many Surrey and Sussex executors proved wills there. Numerous general indexes to the records of this court are available, and are listed in detail in Raymond's *English genealogy: a bibliography,* section 11C. A number of indexes and calendars are devoted specifically to Surrey and Sussex P.C.C. records, and are listed here:

HOOPER, HILDA J. 'Some Surrey wills in the Prerogative Court of Canterbury 1383-1570', *Sy.A.C.* **51**, 1950, 82-96; 52, 1952, 32-49. Late 15th-early 16th c.

CRISP, FREDERICK ARTHUR. 'Surrey wills', *Sy.A.C.* **10**, 1891, 143-9 & 295-305; **11**, 1893, 106-39 & 285-300; **12**, 1895, 83-107 & 194-210; **13**, 1897, 95-109 & 177-96. Abstracts, Prerogative Court of Canterbury wills, 1599-1606.

ELLIS, WILLIAM SMITH. 'Abstracts of some Sussex wills of the seventeenth century in the Prerogative Court of Canterbury, preserved at Somerset House', *Sx.A.C.* **28**, 1878, 180-96.

STOKES, ETHEL. 'Surrey wills proved in the Prerogative Court of Canterbury in 1609', *Sy.A.C.* **23**, 1910, 133-48.

STOKES, ETHEL. 'Surrey wills proved in the Prerogative Court of Canterbury in 1610', *Sy.A.C.* **24**, 1911, 56-69.

STOKES, ETHEL. 'Surrey wills proved in the Prerogative Court of Canterbury in 1611', *Sy.A.C.* **35**, 1924, 30-48.

WEBB, CLIFF, ed. *Index to Surrey wills proved in the Prerogative Court of Canterbury, 1650-1700.* West Surrey F.H.S. record series **9**. 1989.

BAX, ALFRED RIDLEY. *Surrey administrations in the Prerogative Court of Canterbury, 1760-1781.* ed. Cliff Webb. West Surrey F.H.S. record series **17**. 1993.

BAX, ALFREED RIDLEY. Surrey administrations in the prerogative court of canterbury, 1782-1790, ed. Cliff webb. Records series **30**. West surrey F.H.S., 1999.

FARRANT, JOHN, & BURCHALL, MICHAEL. 'Sussex inventories in the Prerogative Court of Canterbury, 1661-1725', *Sx.G.L.H.* **7**(2), 1985, 65-7. See also **7**(3 & 4), 1985, 78.

Winchester Commissary Court

WEBB, CLIFF. *Commissary court of the Bishop of Winchester in the Archdeaconry of Surrey: index to the original wills (collated with the act books and will registers) and original administration bonds, etc. Also, Peculiar Court of the Archbishop of Canterbury in the Deanery of Croydon: index to the wills 1752-1858.* 2nd ed. West Surrey F.H.S. record series **3**. 1992. Alternative title: Index of Surrey wills and administrations in the Commissary and peculiar courts, 1752-1858.

Dean & Chapter of Canterbury

PECKHAM, W.D. 'Intestate administrations, 1559', *Sx.N.Q.* **14**, 1954-7, 235-6. Granted by the Dean and Chapter of Canterbury; list.

Archdeaconry Court of Surrey

WEBB, CLIFF. *Archdeaconry court of Surrey: index to the original wills 1660-1751 (collated with act books and will registers) indexed from the originals at the Greater London Record Office.* Records series **21**. West Surrey F.H.S., 1996. Cover title: *Index of Surrey wills proved in the Archdeaconry court, 1660-1751.*

WEBB, CLIFF. *Archdeaconry Court of Surrey: index to the original wills (collated with act books and will registers) 1752-1858, indexed from the originals at the Greater London Record Office.* 2nd ed. West Surrey F.H.S. record series **1**. 1994.

Surrey wills (Archdeaconry court, Spage register). Sy.R.S. **5**. 1921. Also published as no. **17**. of the Society's publications. Abstracts, 1484-90. Reprint on 2 fiche in folder as *Surrey will abstracts* **1**. West Surrey F.H.S., [1996]

WEBB, CLIFF. *Surrey will abstracts, volume 2. Archdeaconry Court of Surrey, register Mathewe, 1490-1524.* Fiche in folder. West Surrey F.H.S., 1997. Not seen.

WEBB, CLIFF. ed. *Surrey will abstracts volume 3. Archdeaconry Court of Surrey register 'Mychell' 1529-1532. (G.L.R.O: DW/PA/7/3).* 2 fiche in folder. West Surrey F.H.S., 1996. Cover title of series: *Surrey early wills on microfiche.*

WEBB, CLIFF. ed. *Surrey will abstracts volume 4. Archdeaconry Court of Surrey wills. Register 'Heats', 1532-1538. (G.L.R.O: DW/PA/7/4).* 2 fiche in folder. West Surrey F.H.S., 1996.

WEBB, CLIFF. *Surrey will abstracts, volume 5. Archdeaconry Court of Surrey, register Pykman, 1538-1541. British Library additional ms. 24925, 1542-1544.* Fiche in folder. West Surrey F.H.S., 1996. Not seen.

WEBB, CLIFF. ed. *Surrey will abstracts, volume 6. Archdeaconry Court of Surrey. Register 'Tully', 1559-1560 (G.L.R.O: DW/PA/7/6).* 2 fiche in folder. West Surrey F.H.S., 1996.

Surrey wills ... (Archdeaconry Court, Herringman register. 3 vols. Sy.R.S. **4**. 1915-20. Described as nos. **3, 7** & **15** of the society's publications. Abstracts, 1595-1608. Reprinted as Surrey will abstracts **7**. West Surrey F.H.S., 1996.

WEBB, CLIFF, ed. *Surrey will abstracts volume 8. Archdeaconry Court of Surrey. Register Berry 1608-1615 (G.L.R.O: DW/PA/7/8).* 3 fiche in folder. West Surrey F.H.S., 1996.

WEBB, CLIFF. *Surrey will abstracts volume 9. Archdeaconry Court of Surrey. Register 'Stoughton', 1614-1621. (G.L.R.O: DW/PA/7/9).* 2 fiche in folder. West Surrey F.H.S. 1996.

WEBB, CLIFF. *Surrey will abstracts, volume 10. Archdeaconry Court of Surrey. Register 'Peter', 1615-1623 (G.L.R.O: DW/PA/7/10).* 2 fiche in folder. West Surrey F.H.S., 1996.

WEBB, CLIFF, ed. *Surrey will abstracts volume 11: Archdeaconry Court of Surrey, register 'Yeast', 1622-1631 (London Metropolitan Archives: DW/PA/7/11).* 2 fiche in folder. West Surrey F.H.S., 1997.

WEBB, CLIFF, ed. *Surrey will abstracts, volume 12. Archdeaconry Court of Surrey. Register 'Farmer' 1627-1639 (L.M.A; DW/PA/7/12).* 2 fiche in folder. West Surrey F.H.S., 1997.

WEBB, CLIFF, ed. *Surrey will abstracts, volume 13. Archdeaconry Court of Surrey. Register 'Harding', 1639-1649. (L.M.A: DW/PA/7/13).* 2 fiche in folder. West Surrey F.H.S., 1997.

WEBB, CLIFF, ed. *Surrey will abstracts volume 14. Archdeaconry Court of Surrey. Filed and unregistered wills, 1534-1558.* 2 fiche in folder. West Surrey F.H.S., 1999.

WEBB, CLIFF, ed. *Surrey will abstracts, volume[s] 15[-17]. Unregistered wills, 1558-[94].* Fiche in 3 folders. West Surrey F.H.S., 1999-2000.

WEBB, CLIFF, ed. *Surrey will abstracts volume 18. Archdeaconry of Surrey. Filed and unregistered wills, 1559, 1595-1649.* 1 fiche in folder. West Surrey F.H.S., 1999.

WEBB, CLIFF, ed. *Surrey will abstracts volume 20[-22]. Archdeaconry of Surrey. Filed and unregistered wills, 1660-[1689].* 5 fiche in 3 folders. West Surrey F.H.S., 2000.

Deanery of Croydon

WEBB, CLIFF. *Index of Surrey wills and administrations proved in the Peculiar Court, 1660-1751.* Record series **25**. West Surrey F.H.S., [1997]. The Deanery was the Archbishop's peculiar, and included 13 parishes scattered throughout E. Surrey.

K.A.O. *Index wills and admins. 1614-1821 & 1841. Archbps. peculiar deaneries of Arches (London), Shoreham and Croydon.* 5 fiche. Kent Family History Society record publications **690**. 1986.

K.A.O. Index inventories and bonds 1663-1730. Archbps. peculiar deaneries of Arches (London), Shoreham and Croydon. 2 fiche. Kent Family History Society record publications **691**. 1986.

Commissary Court of the Bishop of Winchester in the Archdeaconry of Surrey

See also under Chichester Consistory Court, above.

WEBB, CLIFF. *Commissary Court of Surrey, 1660-1751: index to the original wills at London Metropolitan Archives (formerly the Greater London Record Office).* Record series **23**. West Surrey F.H.S., 1997. Cover title: *Index of Surrey wills proved in the Commissary Court, 1660-1751.*

Chichester Consistory Court

FRY, EDWARD A., ed. *Calendar of wills in the Consistory Court of the Bishop of Chichester, 1482-1800.* Index library **49**. British Record Society, 1915.

FRY, EDW. ALEX., ed. *Calendar of administrations in the Consistory Court of the Bishop of Chichester, 1555-1800. Calendar of wills and administrations in the Peculiar Court of the Archbishop of Canterbury 1520-1670. Calendar of wills and administrations in the Peculiar Court of the Dean of Chichester, 1577-1800.* Index library **64**. British Record Society, 1940.

Chichester Archdeaconry Court

HOTHERSALL, GEORGE. 'West Sussex testamentary disputes in the 16th and 17th centuries', *W.Sx.H.* **53**, 1994, 20-24. Based on Archdeaconry of Chichester records.

See also under Chichester Consistory Court, above

Lewes Archdeaconry Court

HALL, WILLIAM HAMILTON. *Calendar of wills and administrations in the Archdeaconry Court of Lewes in the Bishopric of Chichester, together with those in the Archbishop of Canterbury's peculiar jurisdiction of South Malling, and the Peculiar of the Deanery of Battle, comprising together the whole of the Eastern Division of the County of Sussex, and the parish of Edburton in West Sussex.* Index library **24**. 1901.

ATTREE, F.W.T. 'Early wills at Lewes', *Sx.A.C.* **32**, 1882, 123-40. List of Archdeaconry of Lewes wills, 1541-9.

ELLIS, W.S. 'Unpublished notes of wills from probate registry at Lewes', *M.G.H.* 2nd series **1**, 1886, 177-80. 17-18th c.

LOWER, MARK ANTONY. 'Notes on the wills proved at the Consistory Courts of Lewes and Chichester', *Sx.A.C.* **3**, 1850, 108-16. Brief discussion, with wills of Thomas Donet of Burwash, 1542, and Nicholas Wordsworth of Crawley, 1542.

'Lewes probates 1645-1646', *Sx.F.H.* **3**(7), 1978, 220-24. Of the Archdeaconry of Lewes. Missed in Index Library **24**.

South Malling Deanery

RICE, R. GARRAWAY. 'An index to some wills proved and administrations granted in the peculiar of the Deanery of South Malling, and an index to 216 other Sussex wills', *Sx.A.C.* **50**, 1907, 138-52. The 216 'other' wills were proved in the Archbishops' court, late 16th c.

See also under Chichester Consistory Court, above.

B. *Local Collections*

Surrey

Kingston on Thames

BOCKETT, JULIA R. 'A collection of wills of persons resident in Surrey between the years 1497 and 1522', *Sy.A.C.* **1**, 1858, 180-9. Wills found in a chest at Kingston on Thames.

Southwark

CORNER, GEO. R. 'A collection of ancient wills &c., relating to Southwark', *Sy.A.C.* **1**, 1858, 190-202. Medieval-16th c.

Wandsworth

SMITH, J.C.C. 'Early wills, 1404-1564', *Wandsworth notes & queries* 1898, 25-6. Brief list of P.C.C. wills from Wandsworth.

'Wills 1258-1638', *Wandsworth notes and queries* **1**, 1898, 16-17. Brief abstracts relating to Wandsworth from the London Court of Hustings.

Sussex

Battle Deanery
'Sussex probate records I. The exempt Deanery of Battle', *Sx.G.L.H.* **1**(1), 1979, 28-35. Includes calendar of wills etc. 1657-1857.

Chichester
PECKHAM, W.D. 'Some Chichester wills, 1483-1504', *Sx.A.C.* **87**, 1948, 1-27. From the peculiar court of the Dean of Chichester. Transcripts.

Crawley, *etc.*
BRACHER, PAT. *Transcriptions of the probate inventories of Crawley, Ifield and Worth.* [ ]: Pat Bracher, 1990. Duplicated typescript.

Heighton St. Clare
B., W. 'Wills proved in manor court', *Sx.N.Q.* **1**, 1926-7, 252-3. Notes on wills in the court rolls of Heighton St. Clare, Firle, 15th c., especially of the Rolff family.

Herstmonceux
LOWER, MARK ANTONY. 'On some wills of inhabitants of Herstmonceux and neighbouring parishes', *Sx.A.C.* **4**, 1851, 203-8. Brief extracts and discussion, early 16th c.

Horsham
HUGHES, ANNABELLE F. *Best foot forward: goods and chattels of some Horsham shoemakers, 1626-1734.* Horsham: Horsham Museum, 1999. Probate inventories.

HUGHES, ANNABELLE F. *Down at the old Bull and Bush: goods & chattels of some Horsham innkeepers, 1611-1806.* Horsham: [Horsham Museum], 1998. Probate inventories.

HUGHES, ANNABELLE F. *Head to toe: goods and chattels of some Horsham tradesmen 1612-1734.* Horsham: the author, 1995.

HUGHES, ANNABELLE F. *Hell for leather: tanners and tanning in Horsham, 1520-1741.* [Horsham]: [Horsham Museum], 1998. Probate inventories.

HUGHES, ANNABELLE F. *Hammer & chisel: goods and chattels of some Horsham tradesmen, 1614-1740.* Horsham: the author, [199-?]

HUGHES, ANNABELLE F. *Husbands & widows: goods & chattels of some Horsham couples, 1614-1740.* Horsham: the author, 1995.

HUGHES, ANNABELLE F. *On the first five hundred years of shops and shopping in Horsham: a paper based on 29 seventeenth century inventories.* [Horsham]: [Horsham Museum], 1989.

HUGHES, ANNABELLE F. *Pen, ink & scalpel: goods & chattels of some Horsham professionals, 1626-1750.* Horsham: the author, 1997. Selected probate inventories.

HUGHES, ANNABELLE. 'Horsham probate inventories: an update', *W.Sx.H.* **59**, 1997, 23-8. General discussion, with inventory of Ann Nash, 1639.

Midhurst
WILLIAMS, I.L. 'A first look at Midhurst inventories', *W.Sx.H.* **49**, 1992, 29-31. General discussion.

Petworth
KENYON, G.H. 'Petworth town & trades, 1610-1760', *Sx.A.C.* **96**, 1958, 35-107; **98**, 1960, 71-117; **99**, 1961, 102-48. Based on probate inventories; includes 'summaries'.

Pulborough
RICE, R. GARRAWAY. 'Notes relating to the parish church of St. Mary, Pulborough, Sussex, derived from 15th and 16th century wills', *Transactions of the St. Paul's Ecclesiological Society* **4**, 1890, 135-40. Includes brief extracts from wills.

Steyning
PENNINGTON, JANET, & SLEIGHT, JOYCE. 'Steyning town and its trades, 1559-1787', *Sx.A.C.* **130**, 1992, 164-88. Includes list of 'Steyning tradesmen with surviving inventories, 1559-1787'.

Wivelsfield
ATTREE, F.W.T. 'Extracts from wills for a history of Wivelsfield in the County of Sussex', *M.G.H.* 2nd series **1**, 1886, 249-52, 270-3, 279-83 & 297-300. 16-18th c.

C. *Individual and Family Wills*

Allen
'Lewes wills: William Allen 1692, of Fletching, yeoman', *D.P.H.S.M.* **3**(7), 1988, 22.

51

Andrews

HARRISON, FREDERICK. 'A Bepton farmer's goods, 1577', *Sx.N.Q.* **1**, 1926-7, 120-21. Probate inventory of John Andrews.

Ashburnham

E[LLIS], W.S. 'Ashburnham family', *M.G.H.* N.S. **4**, 1884, 290. Will of John Ashburnham of Ashburnham, Sussex, 1639.

A'Weeks

'Brown envelopes', *H. & R.F.H.S.J.* **10**(2), 1995, I. Will of Thomas A'Weeks of St. Clements, 1563.

Aynescombe

ANSCOMBE, ALFRED. 'An Aynescombe of Mayfield will of 1649', *Sx.A.C.* **70**, 1929, 165-71. Will of Thomas Aynescombe.

Baker

See Dudley

Barber

See Stanbynorth

Barnes

See Holland

Batchelder

BATCHELDER, CHARLES E. 'Batchelder wills', *New England historical and genealogical register.* **47** 1893, 356-7. Wills of Henry Batcheler 1612, Elizabeth Bacheler, 1612/13, both of Wymering, Hampshire; also of John Bachler of Beckley, Sussex, 1602.

Baudouin

DAVIS, CECIL T. 'Will of James Baudouin', *Proceedings of the Huguenot Society of London* **6**, 1898-1901, 172-80. 1738.
'Will of James Baudoin', *Wandsworth notes & queries* **5**, 1899, 84-90. Of Putney, 1818.

Baynyne

MALDEN, H.E. 'The will of a Newdigate rector, 1540', *Sy.A.C.* **38**, 1929-30, 103-4. Will of John Baynyne.

Beckham

PARKS, PEGGY. 'The will and inventory of John Beckham, vicar of Farnham died 1558', *F.M.S.Q.N.* **7**(1), 1984, 4-7. Includes discussion.

Bennett

RICE, ROBER GARRAWAY. 'The will of Anthony Bennett of Chertsey, Co.Surrey, goldsmith', *Reliquary* **23**, 1882-3, 20-67. 1656 (proved 1658/9).

Blaker

RENSHAW, WALTER C. 'Blaker of Portslade', *Sx.A.C.* **39**, 1894, 217-8. Will of Edward Blaker, 1571.
'Will of Christian Blaker of Portslade', *Sx.A.C.* **19**, 1867, 200-201. 1579.

Bothe

A., F.S. 'Will of John Bothe of Thames Ditton, 1546', *Cheshire sheaf* 3rd series, **17**, 1922, 34.

Boxall

See Holland

Brabey

STANDING, R.W. 'Probate inventories: East Preston and Kingston', *W.Sx.H.* **17**, 1980, 1-5. Analysis; includes facsimile of the inventory of John Brabey, 1695.

Bradbryge

See Dudley

Bulmer

DREYFUS, JOHN, & ISAAC, PETER C.G. 'William Bulmer's will', in *Studies in the book trade in honour of Graham Pollard.* Oxford Bibliographical Society publications N.S., **18**, 1975, 341-9. Of Clapham Rise; 1830.

Burgess

BURGESS, RICHARDS. 'Burgess wills, Lewes Archdeaconry', *Sx.F.H.* **12**(8), 1997, 294. List.

Burgh

BAIGENT, FRANCIS JOSEPH. 'Thomas Burgh and Isabella his wife, with a few words on the benediction of widows', *Sy.A.C.* **3**, 1865, 208-19. Includes will of Thomas Burgh, 1379.

Caket
See Ladd

Capron
See Stillwell

Cawarden
J[ENKINSON], H. 'The funeral expenses of Sir Thomas Cawarden', *Sy.A.C.* **36**, 1925, 116-7. Account, 1559.

Chamber
See Dudley

Copyas
ROSS, THOMAS. 'An ancient Hastings will', *Sx.A.C.* **19**, 1867', 196-7. Will of Emmata Copyas, 1416.

Cosens
HOLT, NORMA. 'But where's the Guz - Under??!!' *H.& R.F.H.S.J.* **1**(3), 1987, 11-13. Probate inventory of Richard Cosens of Hastings, 1726.

Court
'Court family', *Sx.N.Q.* **13**, 1950-53, 22. Will of Benjamin Court of Lewes Castle, 1736.

Cowper
HODSON, LEONARD J. 'A seventeenth century account book', *Sx.A.C.* **61**, 1920, 61-4. Account of Elizabeth Cowper of Salehurst, as executor of her husband John Cowper's estate, 1699-1703.

Darell
WIGAN, MARY. 'Stray Sussex parsons will', *Sx.G.L.H.* **2**(1), 1980, 37-8. Will of Richard Darell of Hangleton, 1558.

De La Warr
STEER, FRANCIS W. 'A Sussex mansion in the eighteenth century', *Sx.A.C.* **93**, 1955, 13-34. Probate inventory, 1766, of Earl De La Warr.

Draper
ELLIS, W.S. 'Rebecca Draper of Lewes', *M.G.H.* N.S. **1**, 1874, 365. Will, 1696.

Dudley
PRESSEY, W.J. 'Some Sussex *sede vacante* wills', *Sx.N.Q.* **5**, 1934-5, 195-9 & 232-3. Wills of John Dudeley, 1500, John Bradbryge, 1503, Richard Martham, 1500, William Baker 1485 and John Chamber, 1503.

Duncomb
DASHWOOD, GEORGE H. 'A note of some deeds and wills respecting the family of Duncomb of Surrey', *Sy.A.C.* **3**, 1865, 267-76. Mainly 18th c. wills; includes pedigree.

Durrant
WALLIS, W. CLARKSON. 'A business man's will', *Sx.N.Q.* **2**, 1929, 22-4. Will of Samuel Durrant, of Waldron, 1701.

Evershed
EVERSHED, PETER. 'Local, social, & legal history in a will', *W.Sx.H.* **58**, 1996, 15-16. Discussion of the will of John Evershed, 1840.

EVERSHED, PETER. 'Pallingham in 1784', *W.Sx.H.* **48**, 1991, 29-36. Probate inventory of Richard Evershed of Saint Pancras, 1784.

EVERSHED, PETER. 'The will and inventory of a Sussex farmer', *Sx.F.H.* **7**(6), 1987, 253-5. Thomas Evershed of Rusper, 1632.

Faulconer
'[Faulconer family]', *Fragmenta genealogica* **10**, 1904, 117-52. Of Sussex; wills, 16-18th c.

Fielding
LEVER, R.A. 'The will of Lady Diana Fielding, 1731', *P.L.D.L.H.S.* **4**(7), 1983, 182-3.

Fitzalan
SALZMAN, L.F. 'The property of the Earl of Arundel, 1397', *Sx.A.C.* **91**, 1953, 32-52. Notes on the probate inventory of Richard Fitzalan, Earl of Arundel.

Flemyng
LEVESON-GOWER, GRANVILLE. 'Will of Isobel Flemyng, formerly Legh', *Sy.A.C.* **7**, 1880, 246-55. 1544.

Ford

'Unpublished wills', *M.G.H.* 2nd series **5,** 1894, 133-4. Includes will of Sarah Ford of Peckham, 1734.

Fuller

FULLER, J. FRANKLIN. 'Fuller of Sussex: will abstracts', *M.G.H.* N.S. **2,** 1877, 215-6. 17th c.

STOREY, HARRY. 'An inventory of 1615', *Sx.N.Q.* **7,** 1938-9, 201-4. See also 248. Probate inventory of John Fuller of Waldron.

Gage

RICE, R. GARRAWAY. 'The household goods, etc., of Sir John Gage, of West Firle, Co.Sussex, K.G., 1556', *Sx.A.C.* **45,** 1902, 114-27. Probate inventory.

Goble

'A Duncton inventory of 1622: Thomas Goble', *Petworth Society bulletin* **33,** 1983, 32-6.

Gratwicke

DOUGLAS, M. 'Inventory of Eatons, 1687', *Sx.N.Q.* **16,** 1963-7, 289-93. Probate inventory of John Gratwicke of Eatons, Henfield.

Haines

'Haines wills', *M.G.H.* 2nd series **3,** 1890, 54-6. Of Hackney, Middlesex, Chessington, Surrey, *etc.,* 16-17th c.

Hamman

HOLDSWORTH, DICK. 'Thomas Hamman's will: a Byworth family in the early 19th century', *Petworth magazine* **74,** 1993, 36-9. 1827.

Harvard

WATERS, HENRY F. 'John Harvard and his ancestry', *New England historical and genealogical register* **39,** 1885, 265-84; **40,** 1886, 265-84. 16-17th c. wills of the Harvard family of London and Surrey, and of many related families in the home counties.

Henry

GODFREY, WALTER H. 'The 13th century will of Henry, vicar of Ringmer', *Sx.N.Q.* **6,** 1936-7, 103-7.

Hill

WOODS, SUE. 'What's in a will?', *E.Sy.F.H.S.J.* **21**(4), 1998, 22-4. Wills of the Hill family of Lambeth, 18-19th c.

Hilton

'Hilton', *M.G.H.* 5th series **4,** 1920-22, 254-6. Will of Anthony Hilton of Yapton, Sussex, 1633.

Holland

KENYON, G.H. 'Three Kirdford inventories', *Sx.N.Q.* **14,** 1954-7, 145-57. Of Thomas Holland, 1647, William Boxall, 1754, and John Barnes, 1791.

Holmwood

ELLIS, W.S. 'Thomas Holmwood', *M.G.H.* N.S. **1,** 1874, 366. Of Lewes; will, 1689.

Humphrey

SPURRELL, F. 'Inventory of the goods of Cornelius Humphrey, of Newhaven, 1697', *Sx.A.C.* **6,** 1853, 190-96. Includes pedigree, 17-18th c.

Huntingford

MCCULLOCH, LYN. 'Wills, wonderful wills!' *R. & B.* **18**(4), 1992, 142-4. Notes on wills of the Huntingford family, 18-19th c.

MCCULLOCH, LYN. 'Wills, wonderful wills', *Family tree magazine* **9**(7), 1993, 17. Discusses wills of the Huntingford family of Worplesdon.

Hyland

FRENCH, ELIZABETH. 'Genealogical research in England', *New England historical and genealogical register* **66,** 1912, 61-7. Hyland family wills, 16-17th c., with extracts from various Sussex and Kent parish registers, *etc.*

Ichyngton

RAY, JOHN E. 'Icklesham church', *Sx.N.Q.* **1,** 1926-7, 154-5. Primarily the will of John Ichyngton, 1497.

Ladd

SAALER, MARY. 'Pottingers pothooks & porsnetts', *E.Sy.F.H.S.J.* **11**(2), 1998, 19-23. General discussion of probate inventories, with the inventories of Richard Ladd of Caterham, 1609, Richard Wooddroffe *alias* Sharp of Caterham, 1614 and John Caket of Bletchingley, 1561.

Legh

See Flemyng

Lennox

STEER, FRANCIS W. 'The funeral account of the First Duke of Richmond and Lennox', *Sx.A.C.* **98**, 1960, 156-64. Charles Lennox.

Linfield

LINFIELD, MALCOLM. 'Sussex probate records', *Longshot: journal of the Lin(d)field One Name Group* 2(1), 1993, 29-35. List of probate records for the Linfield family.

Maior

STEER, FRANCIS W. 'Smaller houses and their furnishings in the seventeenth and eighteenth centuries', *Journal of the British Archaeological Association* 3rd series **21**, 1958, 140-59. Includes probate inventories of Matthew Maior of Stoughton, 1657, John King of Shipley, 1709, and Robert Holden of Steyning, 1709.

Marshall

LOWER, MARK ANTONY. 'Will of a Sussex clergyman three hundred years ago', *Sx.A.C.* **13**, 1961, 49-56. Will of Henry Marshall, of Wilmington, 1550.

Marten

'Marten wills: Lewes (Sussex) Registry', *M.G.H.* 5th series **4**, 1920-22, 144-50. 16-17th c.

Martham

See Dudley

Maynard

'Richard Maynard, yeoman and ironmaster', *Sx.G.L.H.* 1(2), 1979, 72-6. Probate inventory, 1618.

Moore

G., A.J. 'An Eastbourne yeoman's possessions', *E.L.H.S.N.* **22**, 1976, 6. Probate inventory of James Moore of Eastbourne, 1710.

Morley

RICE, R. GARRAWAY. 'The testament and will of Agnes Morley, widow, foundress of the Free Grammar School at Lewes, dated 1511 and 1512', *Sx.A.C.* **46**, 1903, 134-44.

Mountagu

STEER, FRANCIS W. 'A Cowdray inventory of 1682', *Sx.A.C.* **105**, 1967, 84-102. Of Francis, Viscount Mountagu.

Mugge

MARSHALL, G.W. 'Will of Walter Mugge', *M.G.H.* N.S., **1**, 1874, 2-3. Of Guildford; 1494.

Newbye

RAY, JOHN E. 'The will of a parish priest, 1545', *Sx.N.Q.* **4**, 1933, 178-80. Will of Sir Mylys Newbye, 1545, of Ardingly.

Patience

BULTITUDE, HELEN. 'Where there's a will ...', *H. & R.F.H.S.J.* 15(3), 2000, 36-9. Patience family of Beckley, 17-18th c.

Paul

'An Eastbourne husbandman's possessions', *E.L.H.S.N.* **18**, 1976, 6. Probate inventory of Edward Paul, 1711

Payne

'An Elizabethan yeoman's will', *E.L.H.S.N.* **17**, 1975, 2-4. Will of John Payne of Eastbourne, 1603.

Peckham

PACKHAM, MAURICE. 'Things unseen and forgot', *Sx.F.H.* 10(8), 1993, 319-21. Discussion of the will and probate inventory of Lawrence Peckham of Mayfield, 1558.

Peterson

SALZMAN, L.F. 'The last prior of Lewes', *Sx.A.C.* **76**, 1935, 178-82. Discussion of the will of Robert Peterson, 1554/5.

Pix

HARDY, A.J. 'Wills, etc., relating to the family of Pix of Hawkhurst, Ewhurst and Northiam, Sussex', *M.G.H.* 2nd series **5**, 1894, 17-19.

Potter

CLINCH, GEORGE. 'The inventory of a Surrey farmer, 1637', *Sy.A.C.* **23**, 1910, 79-82. Inventory of John Potter of Thorpe, 1637; also includes his will.

Powell

MONDAY, ALFRED JAS. 'Abstract of the Will of William Powell of Kingston on Thames in the County of Surrey, physitian, dated the 15th day of April 1639', *Notes and queries for Somerset and Dorset* **5,** 1897-8, 228-9.

Quenell

COOPER, T.S. 'The will of Thomas Quenell of Lythe Hill, Chiddingfold, yeoman, 1571', *Sy.A.C.* **15,** 1900, 40-50.

Robson

L., C.E., ed. 'Inventory of the goods, *&c.,* of John Robson, master of the college of Lingfield, Co.Surrey, in 1524', *Collectanea topographica et genealogica* **8,** 1843, 39-42.

LEVESON-GOWER, GRANVILLE. 'Inventories of the College of Lingfield', *Sy.A.C.* **7,** 1880, 228-45. Includes probate inventory of John Robson, 1524.

Rowed

BATLEY, JAMES. 'The inventory of Caterham Court Lodge', *L.H.R.* **17,** 1978, 36-8. Probate inventory of Henry Rowed, 1764.

Russell

BLAIR, W.J. 'The will of Robert Russell, vicar of Leatherhead', *P.L.D.L.H.S.* 3(8), 1974, 244-5. 1557.

Scrase

LOWER, MARK ANTONY. 'Family of Scrase', *Sx.A.C.* **26,** 1875, 268. Will of Richard Scrase of Halgilton, 1500.

Sharp

See Ladd

Shawe

'The will of the Rev. James Shawe, rector of Ardingly 1550-1558', *Sx.N.Q.* 7(1), 1938, 9-10.

Silvester

KING, H.W. 'Gabriel Silvester, priest (heretofore known as Silvester Gabriel', *Sy.A.C.* **7,** 1880, 272-6. Will, 1512; of Croydon.

Stanbynorth

WIGAN, MARY. 'Stray wills', *Sx.F.H.* 3(6), 1978, 190-91. See also 3(7), 1978, 215. Wills of Mary Stanbynorth of Hastings, 1690, and Ann Barber of Hastings, 1727.

Stillwell

GODMAN, PERCY S. 'Two Sussex inventories', *Sx.A.C.* **51,** 1908, 115-22. Probate inventories of James Stillwell, 1677, and of Elizabeth Capron of Ambersham, Hampshire, 1747.

Stokes

'Will of John Stokes of Southwark, A.D. 1424', *M.G.H.* 3rd series **3,** 1900, 290-1.

Stoneham

UPFOLD, E.M. 'Will of Henry Stoneham', *F.R.* 5(2), 1990, 33. Of Brede, 1738.

Stubbington

PARKS, PEGGY. 'The will of Richard Stubbington, clotheman, of Farnham, 1527', *F.M.S.Q.N.* 9(3), 47-53.

Sutton

WALKER, T.E.C. 'Will of Richard Sutton of Cobham', *Sy.A.C.* **68,** 1971, 202-3. 1539.

Teeling

P., W.D. 'A Chichester inventory of 1653', *Sx.N.Q.* **14,** 1954-7, 243-5. Of Thomas Teeling.

Treagosse

TREAGUS, DULCIE. 'A probate inventory of 1643', *Sx.F.H.* 12(2), 1996, 77-8. Of William Treagosse of Singleton.

Vernon

'Will of Henry Vernon', *F.M.S.Q.N.* 1(8), 1967, 10-15. Of Farnham, 1656.

Walker

JOLLY, M.AIRD. 'The will of John Walker, mariner', *Cumberland and Westmoreland Antiquarian and Archaeological Association transactions* N.S., **45,** 144-7. Of Kirkoswald, Cumberland, and Kingston on Thames, Surrey, 1805.

Waller

HUGHES, ANNABELLE F. 'Horsham probate inventories', *W.Sx.H.* **53**, 1994, 29-32. Include inventory of John Waller 1687.

Walter

'Wills relating to the family of Walter of Wimbledon, Surrey', *M.G.H.* 5th series **8**, 1932-4, 161-7. 16-17th c.

Ward

'Abstract of will of Susannah Ward, late of North Walsham, Co.Norfolk', *East Anglian* N.S., **3**, 1889-90, 379. 1775; also of Battersea.

Wetherden

BELCHER, B. 'Extract from the will of Sir William Wetherden, vicar of Bodiam, A.D. 1513', *Sx.A.C.* **38**, 1892, 196-7.

Weyvile

'Will of Richard Weyvile, 1417', *Sx.N.Q.* **12**, 1948-9, 77-9. Of Rodmell.

White

STEER, FRANCIS W. 'The possessions of a Sussex surgeon', *Medical history* **2**, 1958, 134-6. Notes on the will and inventory of William White, of Midhurst, 1631/2.

'The will of Robert White, senior, of Farnham, 1467', *F.M.S.Q.N.* **1**(9), 1967?

Whitfield

WATER, HENRY F. 'Genealogical gleanings in England: Whitfield family', *New England historical and genealogical register* **51**, 1897, 410-20. Wills, 16-17th c., with pedigree.

Williams

HEATHER, PAT. '1653-1676: the inventory and accounts of the executors of the will of John Williams, innkeeper, of Farnham', *F.M.S.Q.N.* **9**(11), 1992, 199-206.

Wodman

'The earliest will at Lewes, 1527', *Sx.F.H.* **1**(1), 1973, 9-10. Will of Isabell Wodman of Waldern.

Worsfold

'A Warnham farmer's goods, 1670', *Sx.N.Q.* **2**, 1928-9, 86-7. Probate inventory of George Worsfold of Warnham.

Wych

BLAAUW, W.H. 'Will of Richard de la Wych, Bishop of Chichester, commonly called Saint Richard, who died A.D. 1253', *Sx.A.C.* **1**, 1848, 164-92.

D. *Inquisitions Post Mortem*

Inquisitions post mortem were taken on the deaths of tenants in chief, and recorded details of the lands they held, together with the names and ages of heirs. Many of those for Sussex have been calendared in Sussex Record Society volumes:

ATTREE, F.W.T., ed. *Notes of post mortem inquisitions taken in Sussex I Henry VII to 1649 and after.* Sx.R.S. **14**. 1912.

SALZMANN, L.F. ed. *A calendar of post mortem inquisitions relating to the County of Sussex, 1 to 25 Elizabeth.* Sx.R.S. **3**. 1903.

HOLGATE, MARY S. *Sussex inquisitions: extract from Rawlinson ms. B.433 in the Bodleian Library, Oxford, described as inquisitiones post mortem relating to Sussex.* Sx.R.S. **33**. 1927. 16-17th c., provides information supplementary to that in the two volumes cited above.

See also:

ATTREE, F.W.T. 'Inquisitions post mortem, *temp.* Henry VII, James I and Charles I', *Sx.A.C.* **52**, 1909, 100-31.

COOPER, WILLIAM DURRANT, ed. 'Proofs of age of Sussex families, temp Edw. II to Edw. IV', *Sx.A.C.* **12**, 1860, 23-44. Brief extracts from *inquisitions post mortem.*

Gresham

'Family of Gresham: abstract of inquisitions post mortem: Titsey line', *M.G.H.* N.S. **3**, 1880, 85-7, 109-10, 146-8, 186-7, & 216-7. Of Surrey and various other counties, 16-17th c.

Poynings

H., M.S. 'The Sussex lands of Thomas de Poynings', *Sx.N.Q.* **5**, 1934-5, 37-8, 82-3 & 103-4. *Inquisition Post Mortem,* 1339.

Selwyne

'Proofs of age of Sussex families: Selwyne', *Sx.A.C.* **15**, 1863, 211-14. Extracts from inquisitions post mortem.

E. *Coroners Inquests*

HUNNISETT, R.F., ed. *Sussex Coroners' inquests, 1485-1558.* Sx.R.S. **74**. 1985.

Author Index

60

Family Name Index

Place Name Index

69

70